BOOKS

This Book Belongs to

Book 11
Content and Artwork by
Gooseberry Patch Company

LEISURE ARTS

EDITOR-IN-CHIEF: Susan White Sullivan
DESIGNER RELATIONS DIRECTOR: Debra Nettles
CRAFT PUBLICATIONS DIRECTOR: Cheryl Johnson
ART PUBLICATIONS DIRECTOR: Rhonda Shelby
SPECIAL PROJECTS DIRECTOR: Susan Frantz Wiles
SENIOR PREPRESS DIRECTOR: Mark Hawkins

Editorial Staff
TECHNICAL
TECHNICAL WRITERS: Laura Siar Holyfield,
 Mary Sullivan Hutcheson and Christina Kirkendoll
TECHNICAL ASSOCIATES: Sarah J. Green and Lois J. Long

EDITORIAL
EDITORIAL WRITER: Susan McManus Johnson

FOODS
FOODS EDITOR: Jane Kenner Prather
CONTRIBUTING TEST KITCHEN STAFF: Rose Glass Klein

DESIGN
DESIGN CAPTAIN: Becky Werle
DESIGNERS: Kathy Middleton Elrod, Kim Hamblin,
 Kelly Reider, Anne Pulliam Stocks and Lori Wenger

ART
ART CATEGORY MANAGER: Lora Puls
LEAD GRAPHIC ARTIST: Angela Ormsby Stark
GRAPHIC ARTISTS: Dayle Carozza, Amy Temple
 and Janie Wright
IMAGING TECHNICIANS: Brian Hall, Stephanie Johnson
 and Mark R. Potter
PHOTOGRAPHY MANAGER: Katherine Atchison
CONTRIBUTING PHOTO STYLIST: Christy Myers
PUBLISHING SYSTEMS ADMINISTRATOR: Becky Riddle
PUBLISHING SYSTEMS ASSISTANTS: Clint Hanson and
 John Rose

BUSINESS STAFF

VICE PRESIDENT AND CHIEF OPERATIONS OFFICER:
 Tom Siebenmorgen
DIRECTOR OF FINANCE AND ADMINISTRATION:
 Laticia Mull Dittrich
VICE PRESIDENT, SALES AND MARKETING: Pam Stebbins
NATIONAL ACCOUNTS DIRECTOR: Martha Adams
SALES AND SERVICES DIRECTOR: Margaret Reinold
INFORMATION TECHNOLOGY DIRECTOR: Hermine Linz
CONTROLLER: Francis Caple
VICE PRESIDENT, OPERATIONS: Jim Dittrich
COMPTROLLER, OPERATIONS: Rob Thieme
RETAIL CUSTOMER SERVICE MANAGER: Stan Raynor
PRINT PRODUCTION MANAGER: Fred F. Pruss

OXMOOR HOUSE

EDITOR-IN-CHIEF: Nancy Fitzpatrick Wyatt
EXECUTIVE EDITOR: Susan Payne Dobbs
FOODS EDITOR: Kelly Hooper Troiano
PHOTOGRAPHY DIRECTOR: Jim Bathie
SENIOR PHOTO STYLIST: Kay E. Clarke
ASSOCIATE PHOTO STYLIST: Katherine Eckert Coyne
TEST KITCHENS DIRECTOR: Elizabeth Tyler Austin
TEST KITCHENS ASSISTANT DIRECTOR: Julie Christopher
TEST KITCHENS PROFESSIONALS: Kathleen Royal Phillips,
 Catherine Crowell Steele and Ashley T. Strickland
CONTRIBUTING TEST KITCHENS PROFESSIONALS:
 Jane Chambliss and Deb Wise
CONTRIBUTING FOOD STYLISTS: Ana Kelly and
 Debby Maugans
CONTRIBUTING PHOTOGRAPHER: Lee Harrelson

Library of Congress Catalog Number 99-71586
Hardcover ISBN 0-84873-279-0   Softcover ISBN 0-84873-287-1

10 9 8 7 6 5 4 3 2 1

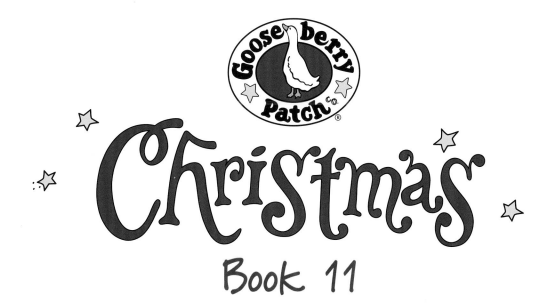

Christmas

Book 11

Christmas

Gooseberry Patch

Sending warm & cozy Christmas wishes
to all our family & friends!

4

How Did Gooseberry Patch Get Started?

You may know the story of Gooseberry Patch...the tale of two country friends who decided one day over the backyard fence to try their hands at the mail order business. Started in JoAnn's kitchen back in 1984, Vickie & JoAnn's dream of a "Country Store in Your Mailbox" has grown and grown to a 96-page catalog with over 400 products, including cookie cutters, Santas, snowmen, gift baskets, angels and our very own line of cookbooks! What an adventure for two country friends!

Through our catalogs and books, Gooseberry Patch has met country friends from all over the world. While sharing letters and phone calls, we found that our friends love to cook, decorate, garden and craft. We've created Kate, Holly & Mary Elizabeth to represent these devoted friends who live and love the country lifestyle the way we do. They're just like you & me... they're our "Country Friends®!"

Your friends at Gooseberry Patch

Mary Elizabeth ★ Holly ★ Kate ★ Spot

5

OH, THE FUN OF THE SEASON!

Whimsical snowmen always make us smile! This year, celebrate all the fun of the freezing season with a few of the frosty-looking fellows. You'll also find tinsel trees, magical snowflake ornaments and a recipe for amazing Caramel Hot Chocolate. The Dapper Doorman greets visitors and assures them they'll find a wonderland of wintry decorations indoors. And if you've never made homemade marshmallows before, a real treat awaits you on page 14!

Dapper Doorman instructions are on page 124.

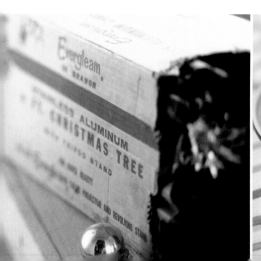

Dapper Doorman

If you could capture a bit of winter to keep indoors, it would surely look like this! The little Snowman Trio is pleased to be a part of your holidays. And the Tinsel Wreath is aged with an easy technique before vintage ornaments are added.

Tinsel Wreath

- fine-gauge wire
- wire cutters
- 12" dia. white foam wreath
- silver tinsel garland
- T-pins or greening pins
- Design Master® Glossy Wood Tone Spray
- 2¼"w wire-edged ribbon
- vintage ornaments

This wreath glows with a cheery holiday welcome. Tie a wire hanger around the wreath. Wrap the wreath with garland, pinning as you go. In a well-ventilated area, lightly spray the wreath with wood tone spray to give the tinsel an aged appearance. Pin a bow at the bottom of the wreath and add ornament clusters.

Snowman Trio

Instructions begin on page 124.

Tinsel Wreath

Enjoy your very own winter wonderland…in miniature! The hollow Snowman Ornament gives you a glimpse of a jolly little fellow and a tiny tinsel tree. So cheery in red, two more snow-themed ornaments are simple to make with paint and beads.

Snowman Ornament

- 2³/₄" dia. clear acrylic separating ball ornament
- 4" dia. papier-mâché ball ornament
- craft knife
- cream and orange acrylic paints
- paintbrushes
- silver spray paint for plastic
- air-drying clay (we used Creative Paperclay®)
- black fine-point permanent pen
- small foam brush
- decoupage glue
- clear glitter

- paper plate
- silver tinsel chenille stems
- wire cutters
- silver tinsel
- medium-gauge wire
- hot glue gun
- silver ornament cap
- Snow-Tex™ textural medium
- palette knife
- mica flakes
- twill tape

1. Separate the acrylic ornament and set one half aside for another use. Center the half-ornament opening on one side of the papier-mâché ball. Draw around the opening; then, carefully cut out the circle with the craft knife.

2. Paint the outside of the large ornament. In a well-ventilated area, spray paint the outside of the half-ornament. Allow the ornaments to dry.

3. Mold a 2-ball snowman from clay (ours is 1³/₄" tall). Press some clay on the inside bottom of the silver half-ornament, making a blanket of snow. Press the snowman into the snow, left of center; allow the clay to dry.

4. Paint the snow and snowman. Paint the nose and use the pen to add the eyes and mouth. Brush decoupage glue inside the half-ornament (over the snowman, too); while wet, sprinkle with glitter. Shake the excess onto the paper plate.

5. Glue chenille stem arms to the snowman. Gluing at each end, wrap tinsel around a 2" wire length to form a tree. Hot glue the tree in place.

6. Press the snowman scene into the large ornament; hot glue in place. Hot glue chenille stems over the seam. Cut away the hanger and attach the ornament cap.

7. Apply Snow-Tex to the top of the ornament with the palette knife to make snowy drips; while wet, sprinkle with mica flakes. Hang your sparkly snowman ornament with a twill tape loop.

Snowman Ornament

Papier-Mâché Ornament

Glittered Snowflake Ornament

Papier-Mâché Ornament

- hot glue gun
- 5/8" and 1/4" dia. wooden beads
- 2 1/2" dia. onion-shaped papier-mâché ornament
- ball-head straight pin
- spray primer
- red spray paint
- white acrylic paint
- paintbrush
- 1/8" dia. self-adhesive rhinestones
- small foam brush
- decoupage glue

- mica flakes
- paper plate
- tinsel chenille stem

Hot glue the large bead to the top of the ornament. Pin the small bead to the bottom of the ornament, securing with a dab of hot glue. Prime, then spray paint the ornament in a well-ventilated area. When dry, paint simple snowflakes around the middle. Add a rhinestone to the center of each snowflake. Brush a little decoupage glue on the top of the ornament and sprinkle with mica flakes. Shake the excess onto the paper plate. For the hanger, hot glue the ends of a chenille stem loop inside the top bead. Make a bunch of these homemade trinkets and fill up the tree!

Glittered Snowflake Ornament
Instructions are on page 125.

13

Yum! What could be better than enjoying a mug of Caramel Hot Chocolate and a plate of Fluffy Marshmallows? Maybe settling under a warm Pom-Pom Throw to enjoy the beauty of your Mini Christmas Trees!

Caramel Hot Chocolate

So rich and thick, you could almost eat it with a spoon!

4 c. half-and-half
3 6.8-oz. dark chocolate bars, chopped
1/2 c. caramel sauce
Toppings: sweetened whipped cream, warm caramel sauce

Heat half-and-half until hot, but not boiling, in a medium saucepan. Whisk in chocolate until smooth; stir in 1/2 cup caramel sauce. Serve hot in mugs with a dollop of sweetened whipped cream drizzled with warm caramel sauce. Makes 4 servings.

Sweetened Whipped Cream:
2 c. whipping cream
1/4 c. powdered sugar

Beat whipping cream until soft peaks form. Gradually adding powdered sugar, beat until stiff peaks form.

Fluffy Marshmallows

A special treat for your little ones…and big people, too!

2/3 c. powdered sugar
2 t. cornstarch
1 c. cold water, divided
2 pkgs. unflavored gelatin
2 1/4 c. sugar
1 t. vanilla extract

Line an 8"x8" pan with aluminum foil, extending foil over sides of pan; grease foil. In a small bowl, combine powdered sugar and cornstarch; set aside.

In a large bowl, combine 1/2 cup water and gelatin; set aside. In a heavy medium saucepan, combine remaining 1/2 cup water and sugar over medium-high heat. Stirring constantly, bring mixture to a boil and boil 2 minutes. Whisk hot sugar mixture into gelatin mixture, blending well. Chill 10 minutes. Beat at highest speed with an electric mixer about 5 minutes or until mixture turns white and becomes thick like meringue. Beat in vanilla. Pour into prepared pan. Chill about one hour or until set.

Use ends of foil to lift marshmallows from pan. Use a sharp knife dipped in hot water to cut into 2 1/2-inch squares; coat with powdered sugar mixture. Store in an airtight container. Makes 9.

Caramel Hot Chocolate
Fluffy Marshmallows

Mini Christmas Trees

Mini Christmas Trees

Make "snow-filled" stands for these vintage-look silver Christmas trees (ours are 10" and 14" tall and came with glittery star toppers). Find a glass container for each tree, slightly wider than the tree base. Using a palette knife, apply Snow-Tex™ textural medium along the top outer edge of each container. Allow miniature marshmallows to dry overnight; fill the container with the air-dried "snowballs" and place a tree on top. Hang miniature ornaments on the boughs to decorate each tree.

Pom-Pom Throw

- ultra soft fleece throw
- yarn to match or complement the throw
- 1¹/₂"x3" cardboard strip

The whole family will have fun making "snowball" fringe for this soft, warm throw. For each pom-pom, wrap yarn around and around the width of the cardboard strip (we wrapped ours until the yarn was about ¹/₂" thick in the middle). Carefully slip the yarn off the cardboard and tie an 18" yarn length tightly around the middle. Without trimming the tie ends, cut the loops on both ends and trim the pom-pom into a smooth 1¹/₂" diameter ball. Use the ties to sew pom-poms along the short ends of the throw.

Pom-Pom Throw

In the Kitchen

It's no secret that the kitchen is the heart of the home…especially at Christmastime, when everyone wants to see what yummy things you're cooking up. To make the kitchen a merry sight, bring out your white dishes to hold oh-so-sweet displays of candy canes and greenery. You can also create an embroidered Gingham Apron, Embellished Towels and a Reverse Appliqué Table Runner in pretty peppermint colors.

Kitchen Collection instructions are on page 125.

Make your Christmas kitchen cozy with Embellished Towels and a Reverse Appliqué Table Runner. Once you know how easy these accessories are to create, you may decide to make extras for gifts!

Embellished Towels

- white dish towels
- vintage linens
- lacy trim
- rickrack
- clear nylon thread
- velvet ribbon
- cotton ribbon

For each fabric-trimmed towel, cut a linen strip 2½" longer than the width of the towel. Press the long edges of the strip ¼" and the short ends ½" to the wrong side. Adding lacy trim or rickrack along the long edges and wrapping the strip ends to the back, pin the strip near one end of the towel. Zigzag along the long edges of the strip.

For the ribbon-trimmed towel, cut a length of each ribbon 2½" longer than the width of the towel. Sew the velvet ribbon along the center of the cotton ribbon; then, sew a flat velvet ribbon bow at the center of the layered ribbons. Press the ribbon ends ½" to the wrong side. Wrapping the ends to the back, pin the layered ribbon near one end of the towel. Zigzag along the long ribbon edges.

Reverse Appliqué Table Runner

Instructions are on page 125.

Embellished Towels

With their fun shapes and cheery colors, Christmas salt and pepper shakers brighten the table all season. If you're lucky enough to own several sets from years gone by, put them together for a merry display. You can also add non-seasonal shakers in matching colors or other kinds of small holiday figures. Another nostalgic item that will stir fond memories is the Gingham Apron. With red rickrack at the pocket and border, this design is sweetly sewn and embellished …and it looks like the aprons Grandma wore!

CHRISTMAS BRINGS ALL KINDS OF THINGS
Love TIED UP IN APRON STRINGS

Gingham Apron

Gingham Apron

- 1 yard of gingham fabric (ours has ¼" squares)
- embroidery floss
- embroidery needle
- rickrack
- clear nylon thread
- coordinating thread

Match right sides and use a ½" seam allowance unless otherwise noted. Read Embroidery Stitches on page 145 before beginning. Use 6 strands of floss. Because the apron will be laundered, knot all floss ends.

1. For the waistband, measure from hip to hip at the waist. Cut a 4½" wide fabric strip this length plus 1" (we cut a 17½" long waistband). For the apron skirt, cut a 36"wx19½"h fabric piece.

2. Cut a 7½"x13½" pocket piece and two 3½"x36" ties.

3. Referring to the photo, measure and cut triangles along the diagonals of the gingham at the bottom of the apron skirt to form a zigzag edge (we cut a 4"wx4⅛"h triangle on each end and four 7"wx3½"h triangles in between).

4. Clipping corners as needed, press the side and bottom edges of the skirt ¼" to the wrong side twice and topstitch.

5. Along the zigzag edge, mark off squares on point (ours are approximately 5"). Fill the white blocks inside the squares with Cross Stitches. Pin rickrack along the edges of the squares and zigzag in place with clear nylon thread.

6. Press the short, then long edges of the waistband ½" to the wrong side. Matching wrong sides and long edges, press the waistband in half; unfold. For the front, work Cross Stitches on the white blocks inside the pressed edges of one half of the waistband.

(continued on page 126)

Sure to become everyone's favorite sign of the season, the Peppermint Advent Calendar is made mostly of felt and ribbon, and it's topped with the family monogram. And here's a new way to display yummy holiday sweets...tuck them into an Ornament Box Treat Holder along with a few vintage-look decorations.

Peppermint Advent Calendar

Peppermint Advent Calendar
- $1/3$ yard of 36"w red felt
- $1/4$ yard of 36"w white felt
- fabric glue
- red and white embroidery floss
- wavy blade rotary cutter and cutting mat
- $2^1/4$ yards of $2^1/2$"w red and white striped ribbon
- 25 peppermint sticks (ours are $3/8$" dia.x$5^1/4$" long)
- $6^1/2$" length of $1/4$" dia. dowel
- 1 yard of 1"w white grosgrain ribbon
- vintage ornaments
- assorted narrow ribbons and fibers
- assorted embellishments (we used photos, tags, scrapbook paper and mini ornaments)

Read Embroidery Stitches on page 145 before beginning. Use 6 strands of floss.

1. Cut a 9"x35" red felt banner and a $6^1/2$"x$32^1/2$" white felt piece. Trim one end of the white piece to a point for the bottom.
2. With the top edge 1" from one short banner end, center and glue the white piece on the banner. Use red floss to work *Running Stitches* along the edges of the white piece. Trim the sides and bottom of the banner 1" outside the white piece with the rotary cutter.

(continued on page 126)

Ornament Box Treat Holder
Instructions are on page 127.

22

Peppermint Snowball Cookies

A cool winter confection.

1 c. butter, softened
3/4 c. powdered sugar, divided
1 1/2 t. peppermint extract
2 1/4 c. all-purpose flour
1/4 t. salt
3/4 c. almonds, finely chopped
3/4 c. peppermint candies, finely crushed

Beat butter until light; add 1/2 cup powdered sugar. Beat until light and fluffy. Stir in peppermint extract. Add flour and salt. Stir in almonds. Shape into walnut-size balls. Combine crushed candies and remaining 1/4 cup powdered sugar; set aside. Bake on ungreased baking sheet at 350 degrees for 15 minutes. Immediately after removing from baking sheet, roll in candy mixture. Cool and roll in candy mixture again. Makes 4 dozen.

Easy Truffles

These sweets freeze well.

6-oz. pkg. semi-sweet chocolate chips
1 c. butterscotch chips
11-oz. pkg. vanilla wafers, finely crushed
3/4 c. powdered sugar
1/2 c. sour cream
2 t. orange zest, grated
1/4 t. salt
powdered sugar

In a medium microwave-safe bowl, microwave chips together on medium power (50%) until chips soften, stirring frequently until smooth. Stir in wafer crumbs, 3/4 cup powdered sugar, sour cream, orange zest and salt. Shape mixture into one-inch balls. Roll in powdered sugar. Store in an airtight container in refrigerator or freezer. Makes about 5 dozen.

Candy Bar Fudge

This fudge is more like a candy bar...everyone loves it!

1/2 c. butter
1/3 c. baking cocoa
1/4 c. brown sugar, packed
1/4 c. milk
3 1/2 c. powdered sugar
1 t. vanilla extract
30 caramel candies, unwrapped
1 T. water
2 c. peanuts
1/2 c. semi-sweet chocolate chips
1/2 c. milk chocolate chips

Combine first 4 ingredients in a microwave-safe bowl; microwave on high until mixture boils, about 3 minutes. Stir in powdered sugar and vanilla; pour into a buttered 8"x8" baking dish and set aside. In another microwave-safe bowl, heat caramels and water on high for 2 minutes or until melted, stirring after one minute; mix in peanuts. Spread over cocoa mixture; set aside. Melt chocolate chips together; pour evenly over caramel-nut layer. Refrigerate until firm. Cut into 3/4"x1" pieces. Makes about 5 dozen.

Susan Brzozowski
Ellicott City, MD

Ornament Box Treat Holder
Peppermint Snowball Cookies
Candy Bar Fudge
Easy Truffles

Candy Bar Fudge

Easy Truffles

23

dear Santa

Remember when your Christmases meant writing to Santa and waking to find bright packages under the tree? Bring back those childhood holidays with vintage images of the season. You can use our patterns to make fun silhouettes for ornaments, cheery framed pieces and other merry accessories. Or create your own Portrait Silhouettes following our easy instructions. We've also included a cookie recipe so you can welcome Santa with yummy refreshments!

dEaR SaNTa CLawS
MoMMY SayS
i Have bEEN a
good Boy i NEEd
5 TRaKToRS and
a bULLdoZER i
LiKE CaNdy
        J. dawSoN

for
Santa

25

Jolly Frame Set

- fine-grit sandpaper
- red spray paint
- 5 open-backed frames with glass
  (5$\frac{1}{2}$"x7$\frac{1}{2}$" opening)
- clear acrylic spray sealer
- double-sided removable tape
- red cardstock
- craft knife and cutting mat
- $\frac{1}{8}$" dia. hole punch
- scrapbook paper
- glue stick
- snowflake punch
- double-sided tape

1. For these jolly frames, lightly sand, then spray paint the frames in a well-ventilated area. Lightly sand around the edges for a slightly-worn look. Apply sealer to the frames.

(continued on page 127)

Girl & Tree Silhouette
Instructions are on page 127.

Girl & Tree Silhouette

Santa Silhouette

Images of childhood joy, the Girl & Tree Silhouette and Santa Silhouette brighten a mantel or shelf with sweet nostalgia. Paper letters, framed between layers of glass, announce the arrival of the "Jolly" season.

Santa Silhouette

- fine-grit sandpaper
- apple green acrylic paint
- paintbrush
- unfinished wood frame (8"x10" opening)
- clear acrylic sealer
- 1¹⁄₂"w red gingham ribbon
- hot glue gun
- spray adhesive
- snowflake punches
- red cardstock
- jingle bells
- double-sided removable tape
- craft knife and cutting mat
- scrapbook paper

1. Lightly sand, then paint the frame. Lightly sand the edges for an aged appearance. Apply sealer to the frame.

2. Center and wrap a ribbon length around each side of the frame and hot glue to the frame back. Using spray adhesive in a well-ventilated area, adhere punched cardstock snowflakes to the frame. Hot glue the bells to the frame.

3. Enlarge the pattern on page 149 to 200%. Tape the pattern to cardstock. Cut out the image with the craft knife. Remove the pattern.

4. Adhere scrapbook paper to the frame backing with spray adhesive; trim. Place the backing in the frame and adhere the image to the paper.

Bell & Tree Silhouettes
Portrait Silhouettes
Oval Word Ornaments
Santa Globes

dear Santa,
I hav ben very
gud thi2 year.

wish

wish

jingle

jolly

joy

28

All is merry & bright on this colorful tree! Portrait Silhouettes celebrate the youngsters in your family. Add even more good cheer with fun Bell & Tree Silhouettes, Oval Word Ornaments and Santa Globes.

Portrait Silhouettes
- fine-grit sandpaper
- apple green and green acrylic paint
- paintbrush
- oval unfinished wood frames
- clear acrylic sealer
- double-sided removable tape
- red cardstock
- craft knife and cutting mat
- spray adhesive
- scrapbook paper
- hot glue gun
- S-shaped ornament hangers

1. For each darling silhouette, lightly sand, then paint the frame apple green. Lightly sand the edges for a vintage look. Dip the paintbrush handle into the paint and add green dip dots to the frame. Apply sealer to the frame.
2. Take a side profile photo of the child, using a white background. Size the photo on your computer to fit the frame; print the photo on regular paper. Tape the photo pattern to cardstock. Cut out the image with the craft knife. Remove the pattern.
3. Using spray adhesive in a well-ventilated area, adhere scrapbook paper to the frame backing; trim. Place the backing in the frame and adhere the image to the paper. Hot glue a hanger to the frame back.

Bell & Tree Silhouettes
- fine-grit sandpaper
- apple green acrylic paint
- paintbrush
- small unfinished wood frames (ours have 3"x4 1/2" oval and 2"x3" rectangular openings)
- clear acrylic sealer
- double-sided removable tape
- red cardstock
- craft knife and cutting mat
- spray adhesive
- scrapbook paper
- self-adhesive rhinestones
- hot glue gun
- S-shaped ornament hangers

1. For each silhouette, lightly sand, then paint the frame. Lightly sand the edges for an aged appearance. Apply sealer to the frame.
2. Photocopy the desired pattern on page 148 at 100%. Tape the pattern to cardstock. Cut out the image with the craft knife. Remove the pattern.
3. Using spray adhesive in a well-ventilated area, adhere scrapbook paper to the frame backing; trim. Place the backing in the frame and adhere the image to the paper. Add a rhinestone to the bell clapper or top of the tree. Hot glue a hanger to the frame back.

Oval Word Ornaments
- fine-grit sandpaper
- red acrylic paint
- paintbrush
- 3"x4 1/4" unfinished wood ovals
- clear acrylic sealer
- scrapbook paper
- red rub-on letters
- spray adhesive
- hot glue gun
- green ribbon
- jingle bells
- red jute twine

Liven up the tree with these simple ornaments. Lightly sand, then paint each wood oval. Lightly sand the edges for a well-worn look. Apply sealer to the oval. Cut a slightly smaller oval from scrapbook paper; apply a rub-on word. Using spray adhesive in a well-ventilated area, adhere the paper to the wood oval. Hot glue a ribbon hanger to the back of the ornament. Tie a jingle bell to the ribbon with twine.

Santa Globes
Instructions begin on page 127.

Letters to Santa
Wish Ornament

The kids' Letters to Santa make pretty keepsake scrolls for the tree, while the Wish Ornament, Santa & Sleigh Tray and Holiday Gumdrop Cookies all remind us that Christmas is for children…of every age!

Letters to Santa
- children's letters to Santa from years past (or white paper)
- wrapping paper
- double-sided tape
- ribbon
- holiday stickers
- adhesive foam dots

    For each scroll, roll a letter, then wrap it with a smaller piece of wrapping paper; tape closed. Tie a ribbon around the letter and add a sticker with foam dots.

Wish Ornament
- fine-grit sandpaper
- red acrylic paint
- paintbrush
- wooden word (Wish)
- clear acrylic sealer
- self-adhesive rhinestone

    Lightly sand, then paint the word red. Apply sealer to the word. Dot the "i" with the rhinestone and you've just made a wonderful "Wish!"

Santa & Sleigh Tray

Holiday Gumdrop Cookies

Holiday Gumdrop Cookies

Christmas just wouldn't be the same without Holiday Gumdrop Cookies!

1/2 c. butter, softened
1/2 c. margarine, softened
1 c. sugar
2 eggs
1 t. vanilla extract
2 c. all-purpose flour
1 t. baking powder
1/2 t. baking soda
1/4 t. salt
2 c. quick-cooking oatmeal,
　　uncooked
1 c. flaked coconut
1 c. chopped pecans
1 c. gumdrops, sliced
sugar

Blend together butter, margarine and one cup sugar. Stir in eggs, one at a time, and vanilla until well mixed; set aside. Sift together flour, baking powder, baking soda and salt; add to butter mixture and mix well. Stir in the next 4 ingredients just until mixed; chill dough about one hour. With floured hands, roll dough into 1 1/2-inch balls. Place on parchment paper-lined baking sheets. Flatten cookies using the bottom of a drinking glass dipped in sugar. Bake at 375 degrees for 10 to 12 minutes. Makes about 3 dozen.

Pat Habiger
Spearville, KS

Santa & Sleigh Tray

- fine-grit sandpaper
- apple green acrylic paint
- paintbrush
- wooden tray with plexiglass insert (our insert is 10"x14")
- clear acrylic sealer
- double-sided removable tape
- red cardstock (at least 13"w)
- craft knife and cutting mat
- wrapping paper
- double-sided tape
- mica flakes

1. Lightly sand, then paint the tray. Lightly sand the edges to age the tray. Apply sealer to the tray.

2. Enlarge the pattern on page 148 to fit your tray (we enlarged ours to 202%). Use removable tape to adhere the pattern to cardstock. Cut out the image with the craft knife. Remove the pattern.
3. Cut wrapping paper the same size as the plexiglass insert. Use double-sided tape to attach the image to the wrapping paper. Place the wrapping paper in the tray, sprinkle with mica flakes and place the plexiglass over everything. This delightlful tray will serve up the smiles.

Keeping Christmas, Naturally

If you usually have a real Christmas tree, why not use a live tree this year instead of a cut one? You could plant it in your yard and watch it grow! To continue the nature-friendly Yuletide theme, decorate glass jars for pretty candleholders and make easy gift bags that can be used over and over again. With Felt Ornaments on the tree and old-fashioned Gingerbread Cookies baking in the kitchen, this natural Christmas is oh-so cozy!

Felt Ornaments & Tree Topper instructions are on page 128.

The felt Tree Skirt is a fun way to dress up any Christmas tree, but it's also large enough to cover the root ball of a living tree. If you want to plant your living tree outdoors after the holidays, place it away from indoor heat sources and water it daily. Only keep it inside your warm house for a few days. After Christmas, if temperatures outside are much cooler than indoors, let the tree rest in a sunlit garage or shed for two to three weeks before planting.

Yarn Ball Garland

Everyone will have fun making this bright garland. Wind a small ball of yarn and glue the loose end to the ball. Make a bunch and thread the yarn balls onto wire. Wrap your new garland around the tree.

Tree Skirt

Instructions are on page 128.

Yarn Ball Garland
Tree Skirt

34

Wool Felt Stockings

- wool felt (⅓ yard for each stocking)
- wool felt scraps for cuff, toe, heel and trim
- clear nylon thread
- cotton yarn (we used red and cream)
- needle felting tool and mat
- ribbon for hanger
- pinking shears

Use a ½" seam allowance unless otherwise noted.

For each stocking, enlarge the patterns on page 150 to 332%. Use the patterns and cut 2 stockings, one toe and one heel from felt. Cut two 5½"x10" felt cuffs. Cut circle trims (3½" and 1⅛" diameter) as desired. Zigzag the heel and toe to the stocking front with clear thread. Use yarn to work *Running Stitch* (page 145) lines on the stocking. Work a *Straight Stitch* six-point snowflake or *Cross Stitch* to attach the circles to the stocking or cuff. Or follow *Needle Felting* (page 144) to apply yarn to the cuff to create loopy "icing." Sew a ribbon loop to the stocking back for the hanger. Matching the top edges and using a ¼" seam allowance, zigzag the cuff pieces to the stocking pieces; fold the cuffs up out of the way. Matching wrong sides and leaving the top open, zigzag the stocking pieces together; do not catch the cuff in the stitching. Trim the seam allowances with the pinking shears. Fold the cuffs down. Zigzag the cuff pieces together along the sides. Pink the seam allowances.

Wool Felt Stockings

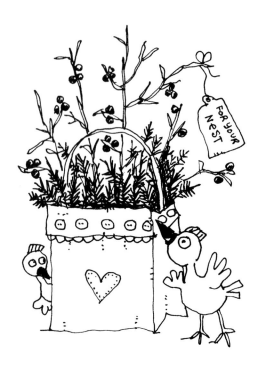

Instead of using lots of gift wrap this year, why not sew these quick gift bags? Everyone will love the idea of reusing the bags for next year's gifts…or for storing items that need TLC.

Felt Gift Bags

- wool felt (⅓ yard will make any of the bags)
- clear nylon thread
- trims (we used ribbon, rickrack, yarn, embroidery floss, 1½" dia. self-covered button and felt scraps)

Match wrong sides and use a ¼" seam allowance.

1. For the brown bag, cut a 9"x20" felt piece. Attach red felt circles to the top half of the brown felt piece with yarn *Cross Stitches* (page 145). Layer and sew ribbon and rickrack above the circles. Fold the felt in half and sew the sides together. Pinch the bottom corners and sew across each corner ¾" from the points. Trim the excess felt from the corners.

2. For the tan bag, cut a 7"x23" felt piece. Mark 2¾" from the corners along one short end. Mark 4" from these corners along the long edges. Connect the marks and cut along the drawn lines to form the bag flap. Layer and sew ribbon and rickrack to the felt about 6½" from the other end. Fold this end up 9" and sew the sides together. Pinch the bottom corners and sew across each corner ¾" from the points. Trim the excess felt from the corners. Using yarn, sew a 2½" diameter brown felt circle to the flap with a *Straight Stitch* six-point snowflake.

3. For the cream bag, cut an 8½"x30" felt piece. Mark 1½" in from the left corner along one end; mark 6" down from the right corner of that same end. Connect the marks and cut along the drawn line to form the bag flap. Layer and sew rickrack and ribbon to the flap edge. Fold the opposite short end up 10½" and sew the sides together. Pinch the bottom corners and sew across each corner ¾" from the points. Trim the excess felt from the corners. Work a 1¼" diameter *Straight Stitch* six-point snowflake with floss on a felt scrap; cover the button. Cut a buttonhole in the bag flap; sew the button to the bag under the flap.

Frosted Jars and Tree Centerpiece

- square and round jars
- self-adhesive shelf liner
- assorted size circle stickers
- paper towels
- frosted glass spray
- foam brush
- decoupage glue
- glitter
- yarn
- rickrack
- fresh greenery
- tea lights
- acrylic paint
- paintbrush
- terra cotta flower pots
- sandpaper
- fresh spruce seedlings from the nursery
- heavy-gauge wire and wire cutters

Don't leave burning candles unattended.

1. Size the patterns on page 151 to fit your jars (see *Sizing Patterns* on page 144). For each square jar, use the pattern to cut 4 trees from shelf liner. Adhere one tree to each side of the jar. Place circle stickers on the round jars.

2. Place paper towels in the jars to protect the insides. Spray the jars with frosted glass spray in a well-ventilated area. When dry, remove the patterns, stickers and towels.

3. Brush decoupage glue over the unfrosted areas and sprinkle with glitter.

4. Wind small balls of yarn and glue the loose yarn ends to the balls. Tie rickrack or yarn balls and greenery to the jars. Add tea lights.

5. For the seedling trees, thin acrylic paint with water; brush over the pots. When dry, lightly sand the pots and transplant the seedlings. Make yarn balls and thread them onto wire. Wrap each tree with a yarn ball garland. We added plain glass jars in various sizes and shapes and used a trio of candlesticks and pillar candles to complete the arrangement.

Frosted Jars and Tree Centerpiece

One of the happiest sights of Christmas is surely a Gingerbread Cabin with a chocolate chimney. And the sweetest scent must be fresh-baked Gingerbread Cookies! The cookies are made using the same fun pattern shapes as the Felt Ornaments shown on page 33.

Gingerbread Cabin

The whole family can help put together this woodsy cabin.

Gingerbread Cookies dough recipe (page 39)
Royal Icing recipe (make 2, page 39)
2 white mint candies with holes in the middle
9 small red cinnamon candies
3 snack-size milk chocolate candy bars (each section is 1"x^1/$_2$")
2 chocolate-stuffed chocolate rolled cookies (4^1/$_2$" long)
3 1.55-oz. milk chocolate candy bars (each section is 1^1/$_4$"x^5/$_8$")
sliced almonds
6 caramel-flavored hard candies
8-oz. bottle white sparkling sugar sprinkles

For large cabin pieces, roll out dough to ^{1}/$_8$-inch thickness directly on pieces of parchment paper and then transfer the paper to your baking sheets. Roll out small pieces on a lightly floured surface to ^{1}/$_8$-inch thickness and transfer to ungreased or parchment-covered baking sheets.

(continued on page 128)

Gingerbread Cabin

BE KIND TO
★ REINDEER ★
WEEK·DEC.
19 thru 25

Gingerbread Cookies

Gingerbread Cookies

Just the smell of these cookies baking will get you in the Christmas spirit!

¹/₂ c. butter, softened
¹/₂ c. brown sugar, packed
¹/₂ c. molasses
1 egg
3 c. all-purpose flour
1¹/₂ t. cinnamon
1 t. ground ginger
¹/₂ t. baking soda
¹/₂ t. salt
¹/₄ t. baking powder

Beat butter and brown sugar until fluffy in a large bowl. Beat in molasses and egg. Combine remaining ingredients in another large bowl. Stir dry ingredients into butter mixture. Wrap dough in plastic wrap; chill one hour.

Roll out dough on a lightly floured surface to ¹/₈-inch thickness. Enlarge the Felt Ornament patterns on page 149 to 183% (or use cookie cutters) and cut out 8 each of gingerbread men, stars and trees. Transfer to an ungreased baking sheet and bake at 350 degrees for 10 to 12 minutes. Transfer cookies to a wire rack to cool. Decorate with royal icing. Makes 2 dozen.

Royal Icing:
2 c. powdered sugar
3 T. warm water
1¹/₂ t. meringue powder

Beat powdered sugar, water and meringue powder in a medium bowl at high speed with an electric mixer 7 to 10 minutes or until stiff. Spoon icing into a pastry bag fitted with a small, round #3 decorating tip (refill bag as necessary). Keep icing tightly covered when not using to prevent drying.

STOCKINGS

If you love the cozy look of Christmas stockings, why not use them all through the house? Holly likes to mix them up, using vintage felt stockings from the flea market to complement the handmade stockings she's created through the years. This year, she made two Felt Stockings decorated with ornament shapes, two striped Knit Stockings and a pom-pom trimmed Fabric Stocking. After that, she decorated the whole house in a stocking theme, from the front door to the mantel. She even created a merry Stocking Pillow!

Fabric, Felt and Knit Stocking instructions are on pages 129-131.

Cheery Winter Welcome

- roll of copper wire mesh (found in the craft store sculpting department)
- wire cutters
- off-white latex enamel indoor/outdoor paint
- large disposable roasting pan
- disposable foam brush
- garden gloves
- pliers
- medium-gauge wire
- acrylic paints
- paintbrushes
- assorted greenery and ornaments

1. Enlarge the pattern on page 150 as desired. (We enlarged ours to 316% to make a 15"-long finished stocking.) Use the pattern and cut 2 stocking pieces from wire mesh.

2. Pour the enamel paint (to a depth of 1½") in the roasting pan. Dip one mesh stocking. After a few seconds, pick the stocking up from the top, allowing the paint to run down the stocking. Repeat with the second stocking. Hang the stockings to dry. To fill in any holes in the mesh, dip the foam brush into the paint and lightly brush over each stocking; allow to dry.

3. Stack the stockings. Wearing gloves, carefully crimp and bend the side and bottom edges to the back to join the stockings. Squeeze the "seams" flat with the pliers.

4. Open the top to allow for the greenery; turn the top edges to the inside and squeeze flat with the pliers. Add a wire hanger to the back of the stocking.

5. Paint stripes on the front of the stocking. Insert the greenery and ornaments into the top of the stocking.

42

Mini Stocking Garland

Mini Stocking Garland
- assorted colors of felt
- contrasting thread or embroidery floss
- assorted sizes of self-covered buttons
- assorted scraps of fabric
- assorted vintage shank-style buttons
- jumbo rickrack

Enlarge the pattern on page 149 to 145%. Use the pattern and cut felt stockings and cuffs. Place the cuffs on the stockings and machine or hand *Blanket Stitch* (page 145) around the edges. Cover the buttons with the fabrics. Cut a tiny slit in each stocking where the button will go. Insert the shanks of the fabric-covered and vintage buttons through the slits.

Arrange the stockings on a length of rickrack. Attach each stocking to the rickrack, sewing through the button shanks.

A stocking stuffed with fresh greenery…what a welcome sight to see! The Cheery Winter Welcome gets its sturdy shape from copper mesh, painted in Christmas-color stripes. And on the mantel, there's a Mini Stocking Garland of felt shapes, all sweetly sewn. The fabric-covered buttons are a pretty way to use up small scraps of fabric.

Stocking Pillow

- ⁵⁄₈ yard of corduroy
- paper-backed fusible web
- 3 coordinating fabric fat quarters
- 3 coordinating scrap fabrics
- contrasting thread or embroidery floss
- 2¹⁄₈ yards of ³⁄₄"w rickrack
- polyester fiberfill
- skein of yarn

1. Cut two 15"x19" corduroy pieces for the pillow front and back.
2. Fuse web to the back of each remaining fabric. Enlarge the pattern on page 150 to 334%. Use the pattern and cut a stocking from each of the fat quarters along the outer black lines (we cut one in reverse and made the center stocking ¹⁄₂" longer than the others). Cut 3 cuff, toe and heel appliqué sets (one in reverse) from the scrap fabrics.
3. Fuse the stockings to the pillow front. Fuse a cuff, toe and heel to each stocking. Machine or hand *Blanket Stitch* (page 145) around the edges of the appliqués.
4. Using a ³⁄₈" seam allowance, sew rickrack along the edges of the pillow front. Matching right sides and leaving an opening for turning, sew the pillow front and back together. Turn right side out, stuff and sew the opening closed.
5. Make four 2" diameter yarn *Pom-Poms* (page 146) and sew one to each corner.

Fabric, Felt and Knit Stockings
Instructions are on pages 129-131.

The fun appliqués on the easy-to-make Stocking Pillow are blanket stitched, and the corner pom-poms are also simple to fashion. For more sewing fun, create a Fabric or Felt Stocking for each member of the family. Or treat everyone to their own Knit Stocking…generously sized to hold lots of little gifts!

Fabric Stocking
Felt Stocking
Knit Stocking

45

Gifts to Delight

If you're wondering what to do for all the folks on your Christmas list this year, why not make these original gifts? The Country Friends have always believed that the best presents are handmade! Thrill a youngster with a toy giraffe. Treat your best friend to a Charm & Button Bracelet. And warm Grandma's heart with a Family Photo Wreath. There's something for everyone, even the family pets, in this collection of memorable and merry gifts.

Family Photo Wreath instructions are on page 132.

Family Photo Wreath

You can easily fashion sweet gifts for young ones…and the mom who loves them! The Jazzy Giraffe is made from colorful socks and has shiny button eyes and a yarn mane & tail. Its whimsical striped legs are secured with four bright buttons. Felt Baby Booties are a precious way to keep tiny toes warm, and the multi-pocket Quilted Tote can hold plenty of necessities.

Felt Baby Booties
- felt
- lining fabric
- embroidery floss
- two $^5/_8$" dia. self-covered buttons

Our bootie is 4" long, sized to fit a 0–3 month old baby. Small objects can be a choking hazard for babies or small children. Make sure the buttons are securely attached.

1. Enlarge the patterns on page 153 to 112%. Use the patterns and cut 2 felt uppers and straps. Cut a slit in each strap. Cut 2 uppers from lining fabric along the solid pattern lines. Cut 2 soles each from felt and lining fabric.
2. Press the inner edges of each fabric upper to the wrong side along the dotted lines.

(continued on page 132)

Jazzy Giraffe and Quilted Tote
Instructions are on pages 132-134.

Jazzy Giraffe

Felt Baby Booties

Quilted Tote

With handmade gifts, you can be as creative as you like. For instance, the Knit Pillow looks special when embellished with a vintage Christmas hankie. However, it's also festive when topped with an antique red, green & white doily. For a gift that couldn't be more welcome, or simpler to make, add ribbon and yarn fringe to a fleece throw. Everyone in the family will want to curl up in this cozy blanket.

Knit Pillow and Fringed Throw
Instructions are on pages 134-135.

Knit Pillow

50

Fringed Throw

Pincushions

Button & Felt Flowers
- marbleized wool felt
- paper-backed fusible web
- tracing paper
- large-eye needle
- 22-gauge brown plastic-coated wire
- wire cutters
- assorted flat and shank buttons
- 16-gauge silver wire
- hot glue gun (optional)
- glass jar with flower frog lid
- Design Master® Wood Tone Spray

1. To stabilize the felt, fuse web to the back of each felt color; fuse a same-color felt piece to the back. Use the patterns on page 151 and cut felt flowers and leaves. Pierce 2 holes $1/8$" apart through the center of each flower and one hole through one end of each leaf with the needle.
2. For each flower, thread half of a 1-yard brown wire length through one hole in the flower, one side of a large flat button (or 2) and through a shank button. Thread the wire back through the other side of the flat button and the flower. Wrap the brown wire ends around a 9" to 12" silver wire stem, attaching leaves to the stem as you go.
3. Add hot glue to the base of the shank button as desired for stability.
4. Remove the lid from the jar. In a well-ventilated area, apply wood tone spray to the lid. Pour buttons into the jar and replace the lid. Arrange the flowers in the jar.

Pick a patch of Pincushions or a bouquet of Button & Felt Flowers to share with your friends. The pretty pins in the cushions are simple to make. Just use jeweler's glue to secure beads on straight pins.

Pincushions
- vintage fabric
- red and green felt
- polyester fiberfill
- sand (optional)
- embroidery floss
- doll-sculpting needle
- $3/4$" dia. self-covered buttons

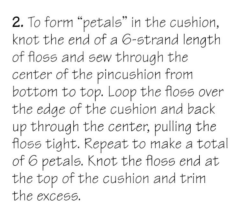

1. For each pincushion, cut a 6" diameter circle each from fabric and felt. Matching right sides and leaving an opening for turning, sew the circles together using a $1/4$" seam allowance. Clip the curves and turn right side out. Stuff firmly with fiberfill (or sand, if you'd like a heavier pincushion) and sew the opening closed.

2. To form "petals" in the cushion, knot the end of a 6-strand length of floss and sew through the center of the pincushion from bottom to top. Loop the floss over the edge of the cushion and back up through the center, pulling the floss tight. Repeat to make a total of 6 petals. Knot the floss end at the top of the cushion and trim the excess.
3. Enlarge the pattern on page 149 to 125%. Use the pattern and cut a felt leaf needle holder. Work *Running Stitches* (page 145) along the center of the leaf with 3 strands of floss.
4. Cover a button with felt and sew the leaf and button to the center of the cushion.

Colorful Felt Birds are happy sights to see in a tabletop arrangement or on a Christmas tree. If you're looking for a gift that will be treasured, nestle a Charm & Button Bracelet in a special gift box. Make lots of smiles by recycling a white sweater into a whimsical Cup O' Snow, Man. And who wouldn't love to receive an entire village of little Glittered Houses!

Felt Birds

Felt Birds

- tissue paper
- coordinating felt colors
- mesh transfer canvas, permanent marker and water-soluble fabric marker (optional)
- coordinating embroidery floss colors
- beading needle
- seed beads
- $^1/_8$"w ribbon
- polyester fiberfill
- $^3/_8$" dia. white buttons for eyes

(continued on page 135)

Charm & Button Bracelet
Instructions are on page 135.

Charm & Button Bracelet

Cup O' Snow, Man

- white ribbed sweater
- 1" dia. foam ball
- white and black thread
- polyester fiberfill
- orange and black felt scraps
- fabric glue
- one 1½" and six 1" dia. black 2-hole buttons
- hot glue gun
- heavy-gauge wire
- wire cutters
- two ½" dia. red buttons
- red novelty yarn
- coffee cup (we used a jadite cup)

1. Cut a 10" diameter circle from the sweater. To form the snowman's head, center the foam ball on the wrong side of the circle. Wrap the circle around the ball; then, wrap and tie white thread around the sweater circle below the ball.

2. For the center of the snowman, work *Running Stitches* (page 145) around the sweater circle 2" from the outer edge. Stuffing with fiberfill as you go, pull and knot the thread ends to gather the circle at the waist. Working *Running Stitches* near the outer edge, repeat for the bottom of the snowman.

3. Fold a small felt triangle in half for the nose. Glue felt eyes and the nose to the face and add the mouth with *Running Stitches*. Glue felt "coal" buttons to the belly.

4. For the hat, run thread through the large, then small black buttons. Run the thread back through all the buttons; knot and trim the ends. Hot glue the hat to the head.

5. Thread a 6" wire length through the center of the snowman for arms. Hot glue the red buttons to the wire ends for mittens. Add a yarn scarf and place the snowman in the cup.

Glittered Houses

Instructions are on page 136.

Cup O' Snow, Man

Glittered Houses

Oven Mitt Set

Family Platter

You will need to size the pattern to fit your platter (see Sizing Patterns on page 144). We enlarged our pattern on page 157 to 203%.

Find a platter (ours is 13³/₄"x19") at your local do-it-yourself pottery studio. Take the enlarged pattern and graphite transfer paper to the studio to transfer the design. The shop will provide everything you need to complete your platter. For a special family gift, have the kids paint the flower centers with their thumbprints and add names with a liner brush.

Oven Mitt Set

Instructions begin on page 136.

Make someone's Christmas baking truly special with a nostalgic Oven Mitt Set! The mitts are made using a thick terry bath towel and a vintage holiday tea towel. See the instructions to make the recipe card, which adds a thoughtful touch when tucked into a mitt. The ceramic Family Platter is a wonderful way to serve up cookies and memories for many years to come.

Family Platter

The family is one of nature's masterpieces.

Whip up some gifts for the four-legged members of your family! Colorful ribbons and a jingle bell invite your favorite feline to play with a Crocheted Kitty Toy for hours on end. And it's a lucky dog indeed that gets to wear the Knit Doggie Scarf. The happy stripes are finished with a stylish pom-pom closure.

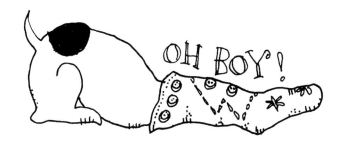

Crocheted Kitty Toy

Read Crochet on page 147 before beginning.

◼◼◻◻◻ **EASY**

MATERIALS
Light Weight Yarn **LIGHT 3**
    Small amount each of Green, Teal, Purple, Yellow, Ecru
Crochet hook, size F (3.75 mm)
Polyester fiberfill
Tapestry needle
1⅝ yards of one color and one 10" length each of 2 colors of ¼"w ribbon
½" dia. jingle bell
20" length of ¼" dia. dowel, painted with acrylic paint
Fabric glue

Gauge is not of great importance; your cat toy may be a little larger or smaller without changing the overall effect.

BALL
Rnd 1: With Teal, ch 2, 6 sc in second ch from hook; do **not** join, place marker to mark beginning of rnd (see Markers, page 147).
Rnd 2: 2 Sc in each sc around: 12 sc.
Rnd 3: (Sc in next sc, 2 sc in next sc) around: 18 sc.

(continued on page 137)

Crocheted Kitty Toy

Knit Doggie Scarf

Read Knit on pages 146-147 before beginning.

■■□□ **EASY**

Finished Size
Small	2" (5 cm) wide
Medium	2¹/₂" (6.5 cm) wide
Large	3" (7.5 cm) wide

Size Note: Instructions are written for size Small with sizes Medium and Large in braces { }. Instructions will be easier to read if you circle all the numbers pertaining to your dog's size. If only one number is given, it applies to all sizes.

MATERIALS

Medium Weight Yarn
 Small amount each of Red, Lt Grey, Teal, Lt Green, Dk Grey, Aqua
Straight knitting needles, size 7 (4.5 mm) **or** size needed for gauge
Yarn needle

Gauge: In Stockinette Stitch, 20 sts and 28 rows = 4" (10 cm)

BODY
With Red, cast on 22{24-32} sts.

Beginning with a **purl** row and working in Stockinette Stitch (purl one row, knit one row), ★ work 5 rows Red, 3 rows Lt Grey, 5 rows Teal, 3 rows Lt Green, 5 rows Dk Grey, 3 rows Aqua; repeat from ★ until Scarf measures approximately 2{2-3}"/5{5-7.5} cm longer than the dog's neck measurement **or** to desired length and ending by working a **knit** row.

LOOP
Row 1: Bind off 9{10-14} sts, purl across: 13{14-18} sts.

Row 2: Bind off 9{10-14} sts, knit across: 4 sts.

Beginning with a **purl** row, work in Stockinette Stitch until Loop measures approximately 1¹/₂{1¹/₂-2}"/4{4-5} cm long, ending by working a **purl** row.

Bind off all sts in **knit**.

Fold Scarf in half and weave seam (Fig. 6, page 147).

With **right** side facing, flatten Scarf with seam in center. Sew cast on end closed; then gather end. Sew bound off end of Loop to center seam.

Make a 1¹/₂"/4 cm diameter Pom-Pom (page 146) and sew pom-pom to cast on end.

Knit Doggie Scarf

Greetings and Gift Wrap

The Country Friends love to share their ideas for finishing thoughtful Christmas packages. Their newest collection of bags, tags, wraps, cards and package toppers is sure to inspire you. So, gather your favorite holiday wrap and scrapbook papers, fabric and trims. It's time for an evening of creative gift wrapping!

Wrapping Station instructions are on page 138.

Wrapping Station

wrap

AlphaBEts

TRIMS & things

Ribbons

BAGS

JOY

The Invite

Why not make gift wrapping an event you can share with your friends? Have them bring their gifts that need wrapping while you provide the wrapping supplies. Everyone will have such fun visiting and trading ideas for making pretty packages that the gifts will be ready for giving in next-to-no time!

Soft Wrap

Here's a clever cover-up. Roll up a blanket, sweater or other fabric item and cut a festive fabric piece large enough to wrap around the present with 6" extra on each end. Tie up the ends with ribbon (pinking the fabric edges if you'd like). For the tag, stamp "to:" and "from:" with permanent ink on a folded strip of torn muslin. Pin the tag to the package and tie on a vintage mini ornament with a bit of ribbon.

Wrap-in-a-Snap
Rickrack Wrap
Soft Wrap

The Invite
- cream and white cardstock
- double-sided tape
- sheer ribbon
- rub-on letters
- oval template (ours is 2" long)
- adhesive foam dots
- striped cardstock

Invite your friends over for a gift-wrapping party! For each invitation, print the party information on cream cardstock and trim to 3"x5". Tape the invite to a slightly larger white piece and tie it up with ribbon. Rub "wrap it up" on a white cardstock oval and adhere it to the invitation with foam dots. Tape the invitation to a 4"x6" striped cardstock piece.

Wrap-in-a-Snap and Rickrack Wrap
Instructions are on page 138.

When they're made with love, cards and tags can be gifts in themselves! Use copies of family photos to make greeting cards the recipients will cherish. You'll be surprised how quick it is to make these original gift tags.

Greeting Card Trio

Let the creativity flow! Use double-sided scrapbook papers mixed with red and green cardstock to make one-of-a-kind greeting cards. Glue or machine stitch black & white copies of treasured family photos to cardstock. Embellish any way you choose (we used a jingle bell, rickrack, snowflake charm, ribbon, embroidery floss and rubber stamps to personalize our creations). You won't want to stop!

Five Fun Gift Tags

Gather ribbons, embroidery floss and papercrafting supplies and enjoy making the perfect tags for everyone on your list!

Joy Tag

Trim the top corners from a cardstock rectangle. Tie on ribbons and a tiny personalized tag (we used a jewelry tag for a pattern and cut it from cardstock). Glue small paper flowers to the tag in a wreath shape (find them in the scrapbook section of your craft store) and add a ribbon bow. Use rub-on letters or write the word "joy" in the center.

Ribbon Tree Tag

Cut a tag from cardstock and trim the corners from the top end (our tag is 3"x6"); punch a hole at the top. On a same-color cardstock piece, glue ribbon loops in the shape of a 4¹/₂" tall tree. When dry, trim the edges into a triangle. Glue any loose ribbon edges; then, glue the tree to the tag. Using 3 strands of embroidery floss, work *Straight Stitch* and *French Knot* (page 145) snowflakes around the tag. Tie a floss bow and some small vintage ornaments to the tag. So clever, so simple!

Gingham Tag

• two 1¹/₂"w gingham ribbons
• fabric glue
• water-soluble marking pen or tissue paper
• embroidery floss
• cardstock scrap
• wired pom-pom trim
• ¹/₄" dia. hole punch
• ¹/₈"w ribbon
• mini jingle bells

1. Matching the top short ends, layer the gingham ribbons slightly askew. Fold and glue the top short ends to the back. Trim the bottom ends at an angle.
2. Use the marking pen to freehand an initial on the top ribbon, or print out an initial and trace it onto tissue paper; then, pin the tissue to the tag. Using 3 strands of floss, work *Stem Stitches* (page 145) along the drawn lines. (Carefully tear away the tissue paper, if using that method.)
3. Glue cardstock to the back of the tag for stability. Tie pom-pom trim through a hole punched in the tag and tack on a ribbon bow and mini jingle bells for added cheer!

Five Fun Gift Tags

Fabric Tag

• fabric scraps
• water-soluble marking pen or tissue paper
• embroidery floss
• fabric glue
• cardstock scrap
• ¹/₄"w ribbon
• ¹/₄" dia. hole punch
• ¹/₂" dia. self-covered buttons
• fabric to cover buttons

1. Center and stack 3 different-size fabric circles (ours range from 2" to 2³/₈" diameter); pin in place.
2. Follow Step 2 from the Gingham Tag to work a *Stem Stitch* (page 145) initial on the circles.

3. Glue the fabric circles to a larger cardstock circle (ours is 2³/₄" diameter). Run ribbon and floss through a hole punched at the top of the tag. Cover the buttons with fabric and sew them to the tag.

Hole-Punch Tag

The kids will want to help make this sweet tag! Punch different-size holes from light green and white cardstock. Glue the circles in a tree shape to a cardstock tag; add a ribbon bow at the base of the tree. Add ribbons and a tiny personalized tag (we used a jewelry tag for a pattern and cut it from cardstock).

Stenciled Snowflake Sack

- snowflake template (we used The Crafter's Workshop template TCW-104)
- double-sided removable tape
- brown gift bag (ours is 8"x10½")
- cosmetic sponge wedge
- inkpad (we used brown)
- scrapbook paper
- corrugated cardboard
- T-pin or large sharp needle
- embroidery floss
- emery board or fine-grit sandpaper
- craft glue
- ⅛" and ¹⁄₁₆" dia. hole punches
- 1" snowflake punch
- brown paper lunch bag
- metal bookplate (ours has a 1⅛"w opening) and brads
- rub-on snowflake, holiday message and alphabet
- cardstock tag (we tea-dyed our 1"w tag)
- round tag
- jute twine
- ribbon scrap
- buttons

1. Choose a small snowflake from the template to be stenciled and tape off the nearby holes. Leaving the gift bag closed, press the sponge on the inkpad and stencil the snowflake on the bag. Remove the tape, wash the ink from the template and dry thoroughly. Repeat with other snowflake shapes.

2. Place the template and scrapbook paper on the cardboard. Pierce a hole through the template and paper at the ends of the dashed lines outlining the large snowflake (if your template has a solid outline, just pierce evenly-spaced holes along the line). Cut out the paper snowflake ⅛" larger than the pierced outline.

3. Use 2 strands of floss and work *Running Stitches* (page 145) through the pierced holes. Cut a scrapbook paper circle slightly

Stenciled Snowflake Sack
Punched Snowflake Sack
Chipboard Snowflake Sack

smaller than the snowflake center and sand the edge. Glue the circle to the stitched snowflake.

4. Stencil small snowflakes on the stitched flake. Punch holes in the branches of the stitched snowflake. Glue on 2 snowflakes punched from the lunch bag.

5. Attach the bookplate to the stitched flake. Rub a snowflake and message on the cardstock tag so a word is centered in the opening when placed in the bookplate. Dot the bottom with glue and insert

the tag in the bookplate. Glue the stitched snowflake to the gift bag.

6. Punch one snowflake each from scrapbook paper and the lunch bag. Personalize the round tag with rub-ons and add the snowflakes. Tie the tag to the bag handle with twine and add a ribbon tie. Glue buttons on all the punched flakes.

Punched Snowflake Sack and Chipboard Snowflake Sack

Instructions are on page 138.

With a few scrapbook and craft supplies, you can make ordinary brown bags, kraft paper and newspaper into thoughtful gift wraps! Create a flurry of snowflake gift bags, or cover gift boxes with nature-friendly wraps. Or transform a child's drawing into a template for easy crayon-rubbed wrapping paper!

Greenery Package

For a natural Christmas feel, tie a layered twill tape and rickrack ribbon around a kraft paper-wrapped package. Paint a pinecone with ivory acrylic paint and while wet, sprinkle with mica flakes. When dry, wire the pinecone to the ribbon and tuck fresh greenery sprigs underneath. Use decorative-edged scissors to cut out a black & white photocopy of a favorite wintry photo. Tie broken sticks together with rusty wire to make a frame. Wire it to the photocopy. Use adhesive foam dots to adhere a vintage tag to the frame and the photocopy to the package.

Newspaper Package

Recycle a bit of nostalgia with a newspaper-wrapped package. Copy a favorite black & white holiday photo and glue it to red cardstock, trimmed slightly larger than the photocopy…on ours, we added pink to the children's cheeks with chalk and a cotton swab. Cut a slit at each end of the copy a little wider than your ribbon. Thread the ribbon through the slits and tie it around the package. Add a colorful rub-on holiday message to the package.

Snowman Wrap

Give your child a piece of cardstock and a pencil or crayon and ask for a snowman drawing or other simple holiday design. Outline the drawing with a thick layer of craft glue and allow it to dry. Place kraft paper over the outline and rub with the side of a crayon. Turn the kraft paper and continue making rubbings until the paper is covered. Fill in with drawn snowflakes. Wrap your package and tie it up with red jute twine and a fun tag. The glued outline can be used again & again to make lots of wrapping paper sheets!

Greenery Package
Newspaper Package
Snowman Wrap

Keep the gift a surprise until it's opened! Create a money pad with coordinating box, or secure a piece of jewelry to a card placed in a three-sided box. For unique finishes, top larger boxes with Floral and Necktie Bows.

Mystery Money Holder
- transfer paper
- 2 double-sided cardstock sheets
- stylist or bone folder
- thin cardboard
- dollar bills
- hot glue gun
- rickrack and jute twine
- embellishments (we used a tag, tag stickers, mini clothespin, ornament and charm)

1. For the wrapper, enlarge the pattern on page 154 to 200%. Transfer the pattern to cardstock and cut out. Score, then fold the wrapper along the dashed lines.
2. For the money pad, cut a $2^5/8$"x$6^1/4$" piece each from cardstock and cardboard. Cut a $2^5/8$"x$3/4$" cardstock strip for the top border. Stack the cardboard, cash and large cardstock piece, so they are flush at the top edge. Hot gluing along the top edge, cover the top of the money pad with the cardstock strip (the hot glue will hold the bills in place, but allow them to be removed when desired).
3. Add rickrack, a tag and sticker to the front and slip the money pad in the wrapper. Tuck in the flaps; then, tie up the wrapper with rickrack and add embellishments.

Surprise Jewelry Box
Instructions are on page 139.

Mystery Money Holder

Surprise Jewelry Box

Floral Bow

Floral Bow
- 1½"w ribbon (5⅝ yards for the bow plus extra to tie around the gift)
- fine-gauge wire
- wire cutters
- wrapped gift

This sweet hand-tied bow will make any girl feel special. The yardage listed will make an 8" diameter floral bow with two 10" streamers. Adjust the amount of ribbon to make a different size bow.

1. For the first streamer, make a light pencil mark on one long edge of the ribbon, 10" from one end. For the loops, measure from this point and lightly mark 9" twenty times along the length of the ribbon.

(continued on page 139)

Necktie Bow with Photo Tag
- 1⅜"w ribbon (enough to tie around the gift plus 20")
- wrapped gift
- deckle-edged scissors
- embossed white cardstock
- word background stamp
- distressing ink pad
- photo corners
- vintage photo or black & white photocopy
- red cardstock
- silver shank button
- paper clip

The necktie bow is the perfect way to wrap it up for a great guy! We made a 7" long necktie bow. Adjust the amount of ribbon to make a different size bow.

(continued on page 139)

Necktie Bow with Photo Tag

Well-Rounded Bird Tag

Extra-special packages will delight everyone on your gift list. Toppers such as a beautiful bird, glittered ornament, vintage holiday record and paper snowflakes are all cheery expressions of your affection.

Well-Rounded Bird Tag

- deckle-edged scissors
- scrapbook papers
- white gift box and lid (ours is 6½"x6½"x2½")
- spray adhesive
- cardstock
- ribbons
- hole punch
- craft glue
- adhesive foam dots
- snap-on paper-crafting fastener (bird's eye)
- twig
- artificial tallow berries
- rub-on alphabets
- glittered snowflake stickers
- decorative chipboard letter
- rickrack

1. Cut a deckle-edged scrapbook paper piece to fit the top of the box lid. Using spray adhesive in a well-ventilated area, adhere the paper to the lid.
2. Cut and tear a 2¼"x5" cardstock tag and tie ribbons through a hole punched in the top. Layer and glue a 1¾"x3" contrasting cardstock piece near the torn end.
3. Enlarge the pattern on page 156 to 125%. Use the pattern and cut a bird, wing and beak from scrapbook papers, clipping the wing and tail feathers as shown on the pattern. To give your bird dimension, shape the bird and wing over your fingers. Adhere the wing with a foam dot and glue the beak on the bird. Add the snap-on fastener for the eye.
4. Glue the twig and berries to the tag. Add a rub-on message and stickers. Use foam dots to add the bird and chipboard letter.
5. Tie rickrack around the present and add the tag...a "tweet" gift in itself!

Vintage Vinyl Topper

Childhood memories will come rushing back when your loved one spots this package under the tree. Wrap the gift and tie a big dotted ribbon around it. Add a twill tape "tag" to the ribbon, using rub-on letters to identify the giver. Find a children's Christmas record at a flea market or yard sale, or dig out one you've been saving. Slip the record beneath the ribbon and adhere it to the package with removable double-sided tape. Accent the present with a holiday tag sticker at the ribbon's center. What a magical surprise!

Snowflake Topper

- white pail with lid (ours is 5" dia.x5"h)
- double-sided removable tape
- red and pink cardstock
- craft knife and cutting mat or small, sharp scissors
- scallop-edged scissors
- scrapbook paper
- double-sided tape
- 1" snowflake punch
- adhesive foam dot
- craft glue
- 1/4" dia. hole punch
- embroidery floss
- wired pom-pom trim

1. Enlarge the pattern on page 152 to 168% (for a different size pail, follow *Sizing Patterns* on page 144 and size the pattern to fit the lid).
2. Tape the pattern to red cardstock with removable tape; cut out the snowflake.
3. Cut a scalloped scrapbook paper circle to fit the pail lid. Tape the circle and snowflake to the lid with double-sided tape; adhere a punched pink cardstock snowflake to the center with a foam dot.

4. Cut a 1¼"x2¼" tag each from red and pink cardstock. Punch a snowflake in the red tag and glue the tags together; punch a hole at the top. Tie the tag to the pail handle with floss and add a trim bow for fun splashes of color.

Glittered Ornament Topper

For a novel package topper, add a glittered ornament to your bow! To place the design on the glass ornament, trace the pattern on page 150 onto a double-sided adhesive sheet. Cut out the leaves and berries and peel the backing from one side of each shape. Adhere the shapes to the ornament, smoothing the edges. Peel off the remaining backing from each shape. Hold the ornament over a paper plate and sprinkle the design with glitter. Shake off the excess. Tie the ornament to the bow with ribbon.

Vintage Vinyl Topper
Snowflake Topper
Glittered Ornament Topper

71

Gifts
from your
Christmas Kitchen

Spending time in the kitchen, whipping up Christmas delights …it's a happy way to get ready for the holiday! It's also a fun way to make gifts everyone will love. The recipes in this creative collection aren't just delicious, they're also prettily packaged. Parmesan-flavored Party Mix in colorful take-out boxes, White Chocolate-Cranberry Cookies presented with a mocha beverage, savory Italian Soup Mix in a kit …these and many other special gifts from your kitchen will be welcomed by one and all!

happy holidays

Candy Tree Lollipops
Lollipop Bottle

Create a one-of-a-kind gift for a chocolate lover by making easy lollipops and presenting them in a candy-filled bottle. Such a merry treat!

Candy Tree Lollipops

We used a lollipop candy mold that makes six 3-inch long trees. We used 4½-inch long lollipop sticks and chocolate candy discs made especially for candy making. Follow package directions to melt the discs. Add oil-based flavorings to the candies, if desired. After the lollipops are removed from the mold, use a hair dryer or heat embossing tool to slightly melt the chocolate and quickly add decorative sprinkles to each tree. All lollipop supplies can be found in the cake and candy decorating section of your favorite craft or specialty store.

Lollipop Bottle instructions are on page 140.

73

Let friends & family know how much you prize them with yummy gifts of individual, Prize-Winning Apple Pies. A cinnamon stick holds each name tag in place. For another batch of sweetness, each jar of Hot Malted Cocoa Mix makes twelve servings of the warm & chocolaty beverage.

Prize-Winning Apple Pies

Smaller than a regular pie, but just as tasty and you have 5 gifts ready to give.

2 15-oz. pkgs. refrigerated pie crust dough, rolled into 14-inch circles
6 apples, peeled, cored and chopped
$1/2$ c. water
2 T. lemon juice
$1/2$ c. sugar
2 T. all-purpose flour
$1^{1}/_{2}$ t. apple pie spice
milk and sugar
5 2-inch long cinnamon sticks

For each pie, cut a 6-inch and a 7-inch diameter crust. Cut out 2 leaves, scoring "veins" in leaves with a knife. Place the larger crust in a 10-ounce baking dish, pressing dough down into dish. Repeat for remaining dishes. Combine apples, water and lemon juice; set aside. In a large mixing bowl, mix sugar, flour and pie spice. Drain apples and add to sugar mixture, tossing gently to coat. Spoon filling into pie crusts. Place a 6-inch crust on top of each pie and pinch edges of dough together, joining top and bottom crusts. Brush tops with milk and sprinkle with sugar. Insert a cinnamon stick and place 2 leaves on top of each pie to resemble an apple. Bake at 375 degrees for about 25 to 30 minutes or until crust is golden. Makes 5 small pies.

Prize-Winning Apple Pies
Personalized Tags

Personalized Tags

For extra-special treats, enlarge the pattern on page 156 to 126%. Use the pattern and cut leaf tags from printed cardstock. Age the edges with an emery board. Set an eyelet near one end of each leaf and personalize with a rub-on name. Wrap the leaf tag around your fingers to give it dimension. Use ribbon to tie the tag to the cinnamon stick "apple stem" on each Prize-Winning Apple Pie.

Hot Malted Cocoa Mix

This makes 5 great gifts!

25.6-oz. pkg. powdered milk
6 c. mini marshmallows
16-oz. pkg. instant chocolate
    milk mix
13-oz. jar malted milk powder
1 c. powdered sugar
6-oz. jar powdered
    non-dairy creamer
$\frac{1}{2}$ t. salt

Combine all ingredients in a large bowl; mix well. Divide evenly into 5, one-quart, wide-mouth canning jars. Seal tightly. Give with instructions. Makes 5 jars.

Instructions: Pour $\frac{1}{3}$ cup mix into a mug. Add $\frac{3}{4}$ cup boiling water and stir to dissolve. Makes one serving.

John Alexander
New Britain, CT

Cocoa Jars

- cream cardstock
- craft glue
- scrapbook papers
- 5 one-quart, wide-mouth jars filled with Hot Malted Cocoa Mix
- tracing paper
- alphabet stamps
- black ink pad
- $\frac{1}{8}$" dia. hole punch
- double-sided tape
- $\frac{1}{4}$"w and $\frac{1}{8}$"w coordinating ribbons

For each jar, photocopy the serving instructions on page 155 onto cardstock. Glue the instructions to the back of scrapbook paper and cut out. Place the circle on the jar lid and tighten the ring.

Use the pattern on page 155 and cut a cardstock label; stamp the mix name on the label. Glue the label to a $2\frac{5}{8}$"x3" scrapbook paper piece and punch holes where shown. Adding tape behind the label, thread ribbons through the holes, wrap around the jar and tie in front.

Hot Malted Cocoa Mix
Cocoa Jars

Pour $\frac{1}{3}$ cup of mix into a mug. Add $\frac{3}{4}$ cup boiling water and stir to dissolve. Enjoy!

Wake them with Cranberry Breakfast Rings...or treat them to dinner with hearty Italian Soup Mix. As a thoughtful bonus, present these delicious gifts along with pretty plates or bowls.

Breakfast Ring Wrap instructions are on page 140.

Cranberry Breakfast Rings

Our pretty breakfast rings make some yummy gifts for those special friends. Wrap tightly and freeze if making in advance.

1 pkg. active dry yeast
2 c. all-purpose flour, divided
1/3 c. plus 1/4 c. sugar, divided
1/2 t. salt
1/2 c. milk
2 T. water
1/4 c. butter or margarine
1 egg, beaten
1/2 t. lemon zest, grated

1 c. whole berry cranberry sauce
1/2 c. walnuts, chopped
1 t. cinnamon
6 T. butter or margarine, melted

In a large bowl, combine yeast, 1/2 cup flour, 1/4 cup sugar and salt; set aside.

In a saucepan, combine milk, water and 1/4 cup butter; heat until warm. Add to dry ingredients and beat until smooth. Add egg and 1/2 cup flour, beating again until mixed. Stir in remaining one cup flour and lemon zest.

To make rings, turn dough onto floured surface and divide into 3 pieces. Roll each piece into an 11x5-inch rectangle. Spread 1/3 cup of cranberry sauce over each dough piece. Combine 1/3 cup sugar, nuts and cinnamon; sprinkle 1/3 of mixture over cranberry sauce on each dough piece. Drizzle each with 2 tablespoons melted butter. Beginning with one long side, roll up each piece and seal edges. With seam edge down, place each piece in a circle on a greased baking sheet. Press ends together to seal. Cut slits 2/3 of the way through the ring at one-inch intervals. Cover rings and let rise in a warm place until double in size (about 45 minutes).

Bake at 350 degrees for 15 to 20 minutes or until done. Bread is done when you thump the ring and it makes a hollow sound, not a thud. Cool completely and drizzle with glaze. Makes 3 rings.

Glaze:
1 c. powdered sugar
2 T. milk
1/2 t. vanilla extract

Mix all ingredients until smooth; drizzle over rings.

Cranberry Breakfast Rings
Breakfast Ring Wrap

Italian Soup Mix

Deliver a jar of soup mix with a loaf of freshly baked bread and all the ingredients (one onion, 3 carrots, 3 celery stalks and canned tomatoes) to make the soup.

1/2 c. dried pinto beans
1/2 c. dried pink or red beans
1/2 c. dried kidney beans
1 1/2 c. small bowtie pasta, uncooked
1 T. dried parsley
1 T. chicken bouillon granules
1 T. salt
1 t. dried oregano
1 t. dried basil
1 t. garlic salt
1/2 t. dried, minced garlic
1/4 t. red pepper flakes

Layer beans in a 2-cup jar in order listed; secure lid. Place pasta in another 2-cup jar. Combine remaining ingredients; place seasonings in a small plastic zipping bag. Place bag on top of pasta; secure lid. Give with instructions for making soup.

Instructions: Pour beans into a bowl. Rinse with water; drain. Cover beans with water; let soak overnight. Rinse and pour into a 5-quart Dutch oven; add 8 cups water, a 28-ounce can crushed tomatoes, seasoning packet, one cup sliced carrots, one cup sliced celery and one cup chopped onion. Bring to a boil; reduce heat. Simmer, covered, for 2 hours; uncover and boil gently until thickened, about 35 minutes. Stir in pasta; heat until tender, about 20 minutes. Makes about 13 cups.

Soup Dinner Kit instructions are on page 141.

Italian Soup Mix
Soup Dinner Kit

Raspberry-Filled Muffins

A treat your friends will welcome for breakfast...or anytime!

2 c. all-purpose flour
2/3 c. plus 2 T. sugar, divided
2 t. baking powder
1/2 t. salt
1 c. milk
1/2 c. butter or margarine, melted
1 egg, slightly beaten
1 t. vanilla extract
1/2 t. almond extract
1/4 c. raspberry preserves
sliced almonds

Line muffin pan with paper muffin cups. Combine flour, 2/3 cup sugar, baking powder and salt in a large bowl. Add milk, butter, egg and extracts. Stir just until dry ingredients are moistened. Fill cups 1/2 full. Spoon one teaspoon preserves into center of each cup. Top with remaining batter. Sprinkle tops with almonds and 2 tablespoons sugar. Bake at 400 degrees for 12 to 17 minutes. Cool 5 minutes. Remove from pan. Makes one dozen.

Muffin Picks and Box instructions are on page 141.

**Raspberry-Filled Muffins
Muffin Picks and Box**

Mom's Chocolate Fondue

What fun to receive a fondue pot and all the fixings to go with it! Keep fondue and fruit in the refrigerator until ready to serve.

6 1-oz. squares unsweetened baking chocolate
1 1/2 c. sugar
1 c. half-and-half
1/2 c. butter or margarine
1/8 t. salt
Optional: 3 T. cocoa cream or orange-flavored
    liqueur
Items for dipping: marshmallows, pound cake,
    maraschino cherries, kiwi fruit, strawberries
    and pineapple

Melt chocolate over low heat. Add sugar, half-and-half, butter and salt. Cook, stirring constantly, about 5 minutes or until thickened. Stir in liqueur, if using. Pour into a jar. To serve, spoon into a fondue pot and keep warm over heat source. Makes 2 3/4 cups.

Fondue Kit instructions begin on page 141.

**Mom's Chocolate Fondue
Fondue Kit**

Cookies & Cream Truffles

These have become a staple at our house every holiday.

8-oz. pkg. cream cheese, softened
4 c. chocolate sandwich cookies,
  crushed
2 c. white chocolate chips
1 T. shortening

Beat cream cheese with a mixer until fluffy; blend in crushed cookies. Chill 2 hours or until firm. Shape into one-inch balls and place on a wax paper-lined baking sheet. Melt white chocolate chips with shortening in a double boiler over medium heat. Dip balls into mixture to coat. Place on wax paper to harden; store covered in refrigerator. Makes 5 dozen.

Sheila Gwaltney
Johnson City, TN

A box of fresh muffins, a kit for chocolate fondue or a vintage cup filled with fudgy truffles...what delicious gifts for the special people on your list!

Peanut Butter-Cocoa Truffles

Let the kids help roll these in the pecans!

1 c. peanut butter chips
$3/4$ c. butter
$1/2$ c. baking cocoa
14-oz. can sweetened condensed milk
1 T. vanilla extract
$1^1/4$ c. pecans, finely chopped

Melt peanut butter chips and butter in a large saucepan over low heat, stirring often. Add cocoa; stir until smooth. Stir in condensed milk. Stir constantly until mixture is thick and glossy, about 4 minutes. Remove from heat; stir in vanilla. Chill 2 hours or until firm. Shape into one-inch balls; roll in pecans. Chill until firm, about one hour. Store covered in refrigerator. Makes about $5^1/2$ dozen.

Marian Buckley
Fontana, CA

Mocha Truffles

So easy to prepare and the taste is unmatched!

2 12 oz. pkgs. semi-sweet
  chocolate chips
8-oz. pkg. cream cheese, softened
3 T. instant coffee granules
2 t. water
1 lb. dark melting chocolate

In a microwave-safe bowl, melt chocolate chips. Add cream cheese, coffee and water. Mix well with an electric mixer. Chill until firm. Shape into one-inch balls and place on a wax paper-lined baking sheet. Chill 45 minutes or until firm. Heat melting chocolate in a microwave-safe bowl. Dip balls in chocolate and place on wax paper to harden. Store covered in refrigerator. Makes about 8 dozen.

Donna Nowicki
Stillwater, MN

Cupfuls of Truffles instructions are on page 142.

Cookies & Cream Truffles
Mocha Truffles
Peanut Butter-Cocoa Truffles
Cupfuls of Truffles

Creamy Peppermint Brownies

Delight friends with chocolate and mint in a terrific brownie!

1½ c. butter, melted
3 c. sugar
5 eggs
1½ T. vanilla extract
2 c. all-purpose flour
1 c. baking cocoa
1 t. baking powder
1 t. salt
24 1½-inch dia. chocolate-covered mint patties

Blend butter and sugar; stir in eggs and vanilla. Add flour, cocoa, baking powder and salt; mix well. Set 2 cups batter aside; spread remaining batter in an ungreased 13"x9" baking pan. Arrange mint patties in a single layer about ½ inch apart on top of the batter; spread with reserved batter. Bake at 350 degrees for 50 to 55 minutes; cool completely before cutting into bars. Makes 3 dozen.

Brownie Plate instructions are on page 142.

**Creamy Peppermint Brownies
Brownie Plate**

No-Fuss Caramel Corn
Caramel Corn Cone

No-Fuss Caramel Corn

So much tastier than store-bought caramel corn!

12 c. popped popcorn
1½ c. chopped pecans
1 c. brown sugar, packed
½ c. butter
¼ c. corn syrup
½ t. salt
½ t. baking soda

Place popcorn in a large oven bag; add pecans and set aside. Combine brown sugar, butter, corn syrup and salt in a microwave-safe 2-quart glass bowl. Microwave on high setting for 2 to 3 minutes, stirring after each minute, until mixture comes to a boil. Microwave for 2 additional minutes without stirring. Stir in baking soda (mixture will foam). Pour mixture over popcorn; close bag and shake well. Microwave in bag for 1½ minutes. Shake bag well (be careful, bag is hot) and pour onto greased aluminum foil; stir and cool. Makes about 14 cups.

Crystal Myers
Hillsboro, OH

Caramel Corn Cone instructions begin on page 142.

Three tempting sweets and a savory snack, too! Whether boxed to go, carried in vintage napkin cones or placed on a pedestal of your creation, these treats will disappear in a hurry.

Caramel Turtles

Three ingredients make a super treat! Make lots of these for all your co-workers.

Lightly spray a baking pan with non-stick vegetable spray. Line pan with waffle pretzels and place one chocolate-covered caramel candy on top of each pretzel. Bake at 350 degrees for 3 to 5 minutes. Remove from oven and lightly press one pecan half into each candy. Allow to cool.

Turtle Box instructions are on page 143.

Caramel Turtles
Turtle Box

Season's Greetings

Party Mix
Take-Out Boxes

Party Mix

A good combination of flavors!

¹/₄ c. butter, melted
¹/₄ c. Parmesan cheese
¹/₄ t. oregano
¹/₄ t. garlic powder
Optional: ¹/₄ t. celery salt
22-oz. can mixed nuts
5 cups graham-flavored cereal
   squares

Combine melted butter, cheese and seasonings in a bowl, stirring in nuts until well coated. Spread nuts on baking sheet; bake at 350 degrees for 15 minutes. Remove from oven and add cereal, mixing well. Cool completely. Makes 9 cups.

Take-Out Boxes instructions are on page 143.

9-Minute Microwave Peanut Brittle

This fast recipe makes lots of gifts!

1 c. sugar
1 c. lightly salted peanuts
1/2 c. corn syrup
1 t. vanilla extract
1 t. butter, softened
1 t. baking soda

Microwave sugar, peanuts and corn syrup in a large microwave-safe bowl on high for 4 minutes; stir. Reduce power to medium and microwave for 3 minutes. Stir in vanilla and butter. Continue to microwave on medium for 2 minutes. Remove from microwave and stir in baking soda (mixture will foam). Pour onto lightly greased aluminum foil to cool. Break into pieces. Makes 3/4 pound.

Peanut Brittle Boxes
- double-sided cardstock
- double-sided tape
- scallop-edged scissors (optional)
- cellophane bags
- 9-Minute Microwave Peanut Brittle
- twist ties
- trims (we used jute twine, wired pom-pom trim and mini rickrack)

Enlarge the patterns on page 156 to 166%. For each gift box, use the patterns and cut a front flap and box from cardstock along the solid lines, discarding the window. Fold on the dashed lines. Aligning arrows, tape the front flap to the box bottom. Tape the small tabs to the box sides and tape the side flaps to the box bottom. If you'd like, scallop the front flap.

Fill a bag with peanut brittle; close with a twist tie and a twine bow. Slide the bag in the box. Close the front flap and tie up with trims.

9-Minute Microwave Peanut Brittle
Peanut Brittle Boxes

White Chocolate-Cranberry Cookies

Cranberries add a chewy tartness to purchased cookie dough...a tasty treat.

16-oz. pkg. refrigerated
    white chocolate chip and
    macadamia nut cookie dough
3/4 c. sweetened, dried cranberries
1/2 c. chopped pecans
1 t. orange extract
1 t. vanilla extract

Combine all ingredients and mix well. Drop by tablespoonfuls onto ungreased baking sheets. Bake at 350 degrees for 14 to 17 minutes. Makes about 2 dozen.

Sandy Bernards
Valencia, CA

Cookie Holders instructions are on page 143.

Friends & family will know you care when your homemade goodies look as wonderful as they taste! Package 9-Minute Microwave Peanut Brittle in whimsical window boxes tied with pom-pom trim. When accompanied by a favorite bottled beverage, each White Chocolate-Cranberry Cookie is a complete snack.

White Chocolate-Cranberry Cookies
Cookie Holders

Tried and TruE

Surely nothing brings back wonderful memories of Christmas like scrumptious recipes…tried & true, handed-down favorites. Why not serve those family classics this year for your family to enjoy? The young folks will discover the flavors of Christmas Ambrosia, Stuffed Turkey Roll and Pear-Walnut Salad for the first time, while everyone else will be happy to see these dishes on the dining table once again!

Pear-Walnut Salad

The natural sweetness of the pears plays off the tang of the blue cheese perfectly.

4 c. mixed salad greens, torn and tightly packed
2 ripe red pears, cored and sliced
1¹/₂ c. walnut halves, toasted
2 oz. crumbled blue cheese

Combine all ingredients in a large bowl; toss gently. Pour dressing over salad mixture just before serving; toss. Makes 5 servings.

Dressing:
¹/₂ c. olive oil
¹/₄ c. sugar
3 T. white vinegar
¹/₂ t. celery seed
¹/₄ t. salt

Combine all ingredients in a jar; cover and shake vigorously. Makes one cup.

Scalloped Potato Duo
Smothered Green Beans
Grandma's Holiday Stuffing
Stuffed Turkey Roll

Grandma's Holiday Stuffing

Apples keep this stuffing moist.

1 large loaf day-old bread, torn
Optional: 4 day-old corn muffins,
    broken up
1/2 c. butter
1 onion, diced
3 stalks celery, diced
1/2 c. sliced mushrooms
2 tart apples, cored and diced
1/2 c. walnuts, coarsely chopped
1/2 c. raisins
3/4 c. water or chicken broth

1/2 to 1 T. poultry seasoning
2 t. dried parsley
salt and pepper to taste

Place torn bread in a large baking dish; mix in muffins, if using (you should have about 12 cups of the bread and muffin mixture). Bake at 250 degrees for about 30 minutes or until dried out; set aside.

Melt butter over low heat in a large skillet; sauté onion, celery and mushrooms until tender. Add apples, walnuts and raisins; stir to coat with butter. Mix in water or chicken broth and seasonings; pour over bread and toss to moisten. Add a little more water or chicken broth if bread is very dry. Spread stuffing in a lightly greased 13"x9" baking pan and bake at 350 degrees for 30 to 40 minutes. (Or use to stuff a 12 to 15-pound turkey before roasting; do not overstuff.) Makes 10 to 12 servings.

Wendy Lee Paffenroth
Pine Island, NY

ELF stockings

Raisins and apples lend a little sweetness to Grandma's Holiday Stuffing, while Smothered Green Beans pack all the rich flavor of bacon and tomatoes. Everyone's heard of sausage stuffing, but Stuffed Turkey Roll offers an updated version with spinach and garlic.

Smothered Green Beans
Lots of wonderful flavors in these beans.

1 lb. green beans
6 bacon slices
3 stalks celery, chopped
1 onion, chopped
1 red pepper, chopped
3 plum tomatoes, seeded and chopped
2 cloves garlic, minced
1½ t. salt
½ t. dried thyme
½ t. dried basil
½ t. paprika
¼ t. pepper

Cook green beans in boiling water to cover for 6 to 8 minutes or until crisp-tender. Drain and place in ice water to stop the cooking process. (This can be done 2 days ahead of time.)

Cook bacon in a large skillet until crisp; remove bacon and drain on paper towels, reserving 2 tablespoons drippings in skillet. Crumble bacon and set aside. Cook celery, onion and red pepper in hot drippings in skillet over medium-high heat for 5 minutes. Add green beans and remaining ingredients; cook, stirring often, until heated through. Sprinkle bacon on top. Makes 6 to 8 servings.

Stuffed Turkey Roll
This gives turkey a whole new look!

12 oz. ground pork
10-oz. pkg. frozen chopped spinach, thawed and well drained
½ c. soft breadcrumbs
⅓ c. onion, minced
1 egg, beaten
2 cloves garlic, minced
¾ t. dried thyme
¾ t. dried rosemary, crushed
1½ t. salt, divided
1 t. pepper, divided
3-lb. boneless turkey breast
2 T. butter or margarine
2 T. vegetable oil

Combine first 8 ingredients. Stir in ½ teaspoon salt and ½ teaspoon pepper; set aside.

Lay turkey breast flat on wax paper, skin side down. Trim fat, keeping skin intact. From center, slice horizontally (parallel with skin) through thickest part of each side of breast almost to outer edge; flip cut piece and breast fillets over to enlarge breast. Pound breast to flatten and to form a more even thickness.

Spoon stuffing mixture in center of width of turkey breast, leaving a 2-inch border at sides. Fold in sides of turkey breast over filling; roll up turkey breast over filling, starting from bottom. (Roll should be 12 to 14 inches long.) Tie turkey breast roll securely in several places with heavy string. Sprinkle with remaining one teaspoon salt and ½ teaspoon pepper. Brown turkey in large roasting pan in butter and oil over medium-high heat, turning frequently, for 10 minutes or until browned. Insert meat thermometer, making sure tip touches meat of turkey. Bake at 375 degrees for 50 to 55 minutes or until thermometer registers 165 degrees, basting often. Let stand 10 minutes before slicing. Makes 10 servings.

Smothered Green Beans

Scalloped Potato Duo
(shown on page 86)
Two types of potato, nutty Gruyère cheese and salty ham give this dish unusual appeal.

1 onion, chopped
1 T. vegetable oil
3 cloves garlic, minced
2 sweet potatoes (about 1½ lbs.), peeled and cut into ¼-inch slices
2 baking potatoes (about 1½ lbs.), peeled and cut into ¼-inch slices
½ c. all-purpose flour
1 t. salt
¼ t. pepper
2 c. ham, chopped
8 oz. Gruyère cheese, shredded and divided
1½ c. whipping cream
2 T. butter, cut into pieces

Sauté onion in oil over medium-high heat 5 minutes. Add garlic; cook 30 seconds. Remove pan from heat; set aside.

Place potatoes in a large bowl. Combine flour, salt and pepper; sprinkle over potatoes, tossing to coat. Arrange half of potato mixture in a greased 13"x9" baking dish or 3-quart gratin dish. Top with onion mixture, ham and one cup cheese. Top with remaining potato mixture. Pour cream over potato mixture. Dot with butter and cover with aluminum foil. Bake at 400 degrees for 50 minutes. Uncover, top with remaining one cup cheese and bake 20 more minutes or until potatoes are tender and cheese is browned. Let stand 10 minutes before serving. Makes 6 servings.

Whole Wheat Spirals
Delicious and has a little different look.

2 pkgs. active dry yeast
1¾ c. warm water
½ c. sugar
2 t. salt
½ c. butter or margarine, melted and divided
1 egg, lightly beaten
2¼ c. whole wheat flour
2¼ to 2½ c. all-purpose flour

Combine yeast and warm water in a 2-cup liquid measuring cup; let stand 5 minutes.

Combine yeast mixture, sugar, salt, ¼ cup melted butter, egg and whole wheat flour in a large mixing bowl; beat until well blended. Gradually stir in enough all-purpose flour to make a soft dough.

Turn dough out onto a well-floured surface and knead until smooth and elastic (about 5 minutes). Place in a well-greased bowl, turning to grease top. Cover and let rise in a warm place (85 degrees), free from drafts, 30 minutes or until double in bulk.

Punch dough down and divide in half; shape each portion into a 14x7-inch rectangle. Cut each rectangle into twelve 7x1-inch strips. Roll each strip into a spiral and place in well-greased muffin pans. Cover and let rise in a warm place, free from drafts, 20 minutes or until double in bulk.

Bake at 350 degrees for 20 to 25 minutes or until golden. Remove from pans and cool on wire racks. Brush with remaining ¼ cup melted butter. Makes 2 dozen.

Whole Wheat Spirals

You can keep your hungry crowd from raiding the kitchen before dinner by letting them snack on Hot Smoky Pecans. There's a surprise ingredient in the cheesy Scalloped Potato Duo...sweet potatoes! Whole Wheat Spirals are almost too pretty to eat, but no one will be able to resist their fresh-baked fragrance. Once the dinner plates are cleared away, it's time for a serving of Christmas Ambrosia.

Hot Smoky Pecans

Here's a little something to munch on before dinner.

1/4 c. butter or margarine, melted
2 T. soy sauce
1 T. Worcestershire sauce
1/2 t. hot sauce
2 c. pecan halves

Stir together all ingredients; spread pecans in a single layer in a 15"x10" jellyroll pan. Bake at 300 degrees for 25 minutes or until toasted, stirring 3 times. Makes 2 cups.

Christmas Ambrosia

What is Christmas without ambrosia? In Greek mythology it was the food of the gods on Mt. Olympus!

12 navel oranges
20-oz. can crushed pineapple, undrained
2 c. fresh coconut, grated

Peel and section oranges, catching juice in a large nonmetal bowl. Add orange sections, pineapple and coconut to juice; toss gently. Cover and chill thoroughly. Makes 6 to 8 servings.

Hot Smoky Pecans

Christmas Ambrosia

The moist layers of cake, filling and frosting in Triple Chocolate Ecstasy are oh-so good with the spicy flavor of Cheery Christmas Coffee. And Pumpkin Cheesecake with Ginger Cream Topping is the perfect blend of seasonal flavors!

Cheery Christmas Coffee
Triple Chocolate Ecstasy

Triple Chocolate Ecstasy

This cake will satisfy the chocolate lovers in your family.

4 1-oz. sqs. semi-sweet baking
    chocolate
1/2 c. butter or margarine
1 c. pecans, finely chopped
2 c. sugar
2 eggs, lightly beaten
1 1/2 c. all-purpose flour
1 t. baking powder
1/2 t. salt
1 1/2 c. milk
1 t. vanilla extract

Grease two 9" round cake pans; line with wax paper. Grease wax paper; set aside.

Combine chocolate and butter in top of a double boiler; bring water to a boil. Reduce heat to low; cook until chocolate melts. Add pecans; stir well. Remove from heat.

Combine sugar and eggs. Stir in chocolate mixture. Combine flour, baking powder and salt; add to chocolate mixture alternately with milk, beginning and ending with flour mixture. Stir in vanilla. Pour batter into prepared pans. Bake at 350 degrees for 45 to 48 minutes or until a wooden pick inserted in center comes out clean. Cool in pans on wire racks 5 minutes; remove from pans and let cool completely on wire racks.

Spread filling between layers of cake. Spread frosting on top and sides of cake. Makes 12 servings.

Chocolate Filling:
4 1-oz. sqs. semi-sweet baking
    chocolate
1/4 c. butter or margarine
1/2 c. powdered sugar, sifted
1/3 c. milk

Combine chocolate and butter in top of a double boiler; bring water to a boil. Reduce heat to low; cook until chocolate melts. Gradually add powdered sugar alternately with milk, beginning and ending with powdered sugar; stir until smooth. Cover and chill 30 minutes or until spreading consistency.

Chocolate Frosting:
2 c. whipping cream
1 c. powdered sugar, sifted
2/3 c. baking cocoa, sifted
1 t. vanilla extract

Combine all ingredients in a bowl; beat at high speed with a mixer until stiff peaks form. Chill 30 minutes.

Cheery Christmas Coffee

Spiced coffee with a surprising orange twist!

1/3 c. ground coffee
1/2 t. cinnamon
1/8 t. ground cloves
1/4 c. orange marmalade
3 c. water
Optional: sugar

Place coffee, cinnamon and cloves in filter in brew basket of coffee maker. Place marmalade in empty coffee pot. Brew coffee as usual with water. When brewing is complete, mix well. Pour into coffee mugs; serve with sugar, if desired. Makes 6 servings.

Kay Marone
Des Moines, IA

Pumpkin Cheesecake with Ginger Cream Topping

This one will become a "must-have-every-year" recipe.

3/4 c. sugar, divided
3/4 c. brown sugar, firmly packed
   and divided
3/4 c. graham cracker crumbs
1/2 c. pecans, finely chopped
1/4 c. butter or margarine, melted
16-oz. can pumpkin
1 t. vanilla extract
1 T. all-purpose flour
1 1/2 t. cinnamon
1/2 t. ground ginger
1/2 t. nutmeg
1/4 t. salt
3 8-oz. pkgs. cream cheese,
   softened
3 eggs
Garnish: chopped pecans

Combine 1/4 cup sugar, 1/4 cup brown sugar, graham cracker crumbs, 1/2 cup pecans and butter; press in bottom and one inch up sides of a lightly greased 9" springform pan. Cover and chill one hour.

Combine remaining 1/2 cup sugar, 1/2 cup brown sugar, pumpkin, vanilla and next 5 ingredients; set aside.

Beat cream cheese at medium speed until creamy. Add pumpkin mixture, beating well. Add eggs, one at a time, beating after each addition. Pour mixture into prepared crust. Bake at 350 degrees for 55 minutes. Cool completely in pan on a wire rack.

Spoon topping over cheesecake. Cover and chill at least 8 hours. To serve, carefully remove sides of springform pan; garnish cheesecake, if desired. Makes 16 servings.

Ginger Cream Topping:
1 c. whipping cream
1 c. sour cream
2 T. sugar
1/4 c. crystallized ginger, minced
3 T. dark rum or 1 t. rum extract
1/2 t. vanilla extract

Combine first 3 ingredients in a bowl; beat at high speed until soft peaks form. Fold in ginger, rum and vanilla.

Pumpkin Cheesecake with Ginger Cream Topping

Friendship Tea

Looking for a new way to get your friends together for Christmas? Try hosting an old-fashioned tea party! The simple goodness of cake, cookies and finger sandwiches go great with conversation. And you don't have to limit your beverages to just tea. Friendship Sip Mix is a sweet complement to Ginger Crinkles and Victorian Jam Cake. Or pair Iced Shortbread Cookies with Dreamy Hot Chocolate. Everyone will want your recipes!

Victorian Jam Cake

Victorian Jam Cake
A favorite of Queen Victoria (and Kate)!

1½ c. all-purpose flour
1½ t. baking powder
2 to 3 t. lemon zest, finely grated
½ t. salt
¾ c. butter or margarine,
   softened
¾ c. sugar
3 eggs
¾ c. seedless strawberry jam
powdered sugar
Garnish: fresh strawberry

Combine flour, baking powder, lemon zest and salt; set aside.

Blend butter and sugar together until light and fluffy. Add eggs, one at a time, beating well after each addition.

Stir in flour mixture. Spread batter evenly into 2 greased 8" round cake pans. Bake at 350 degrees for 18 to 20 minutes. (Cake should spring back when touched lightly.)

Cool in pans for 10 minutes, then invert onto wire racks to cool completely. Assemble cake on serving plate by putting layers together with strawberry jam in between. Sprinkle with powdered sugar. Garnish, if desired. Makes 8 servings.

Pecan-Stuffed Dates with Bacon

Sherried Shrimp Sandwiches
Yummy sandwiches for a tea.

1¹/₂ lbs. unpeeled, small fresh
    shrimp
3-oz. pkg. shrimp, crawfish and
    crab boil
4-oz. pkg. crumbled blue cheese,
    softened
4 oz. cream cheese (¹/₂ of an 8-oz.
    pkg.), softened
Optional: ¹/₄ c. sherry
5 green onions, minced
¹/₂ c. celery, diced
¹/₂ c. walnuts, finely chopped and
    toasted
¹/₂ t. seasoned salt
¹/₄ t. red pepper
112 party pumpernickel bread slices
Garnish: fresh dill sprigs

    Cook shrimp using seafood boil
according to package directions;
drain. Peel shrimp and devein, if
desired. Chop shrimp.
    Stir together shrimp, blue
cheese and next 7 ingredients.
Spread about one tablespoon filling
on each of 56 bread slices. Top
each with another bread slice. Cut
sandwiches in half diagonally.
    Garnish, if desired. Store
sandwiches covered with a damp
paper towel in an airtight container
in refrigerator. Makes 56 servings.

Your guests will feel oh-so
special while enjoying these
dainty hors d'oeuvres.
Pecan-Stuffed Dates with
Bacon are yummy and truly
easy to make. Create finger
sandwiches with savory shrimp
or turkey filling. And the
Vegetable Canapés are sure to
disappear in a hurry!

Pecan-Stuffed Dates with Bacon
Super quick and easy to make!

15 pecan halves
15 seedless dates
15 slices precooked packaged
    bacon

    Heat pecan halves in a small
non-stick skillet over medium-low
heat, stirring often, 2 or 3 minutes
or until toasted. Cut a lengthwise
slit down the center of dates.
Stuff one pecan half in each date,
and wrap each with one slice of
bacon. Bake at 425 degrees for
8 minutes or until bacon is crisp.
Makes 15.

Turkey-Watercress-&-Cranberry Sandwiches

A good combination of flavors.

2½ c. cooked turkey, diced
¾ c. sweetened, dried cranberries,
    chopped
1 bunch fresh watercress, torn
8-oz. pkg. cream cheese, softened
½ t. seasoned salt
¼ t. pepper
96 party pumpernickel bread slices,
    crusts trimmed
Garnish: fresh parsley leaves

Stir first 6 ingredients together.
Spread about one tablespoon filling on
each of 48 bread slices. Top each with
another bread slice.

Garnish, if desired. Store sandwiches
covered with a damp paper towel in an
airtight container in the refrigerator.
Makes 4 dozen.

Vegetable Canapés

*The pretty toppings are cut using
a mandoline.*

3-oz. pkg. cream cheese, softened
3 T. frozen minced chives
3 T. sour cream
1 t. dried dillweed
¼ t. garlic salt
⅛ t. white pepper
16 thin white bread slices
16 thin whole wheat bread slices
Toppings: thinly sliced cucumber,
    squash or radishes, shredded
    carrots, sliced cherry tomatoes,
    fresh parsley, dill sprigs

Beat cream cheese at medium speed
with an electric mixer until fluffy. Stir in
chives and next 4 ingredients; set aside.
Cut a 2-inch round from each bread slice.
Keep rounds covered with damp paper
towels before assembling to prevent
drying out.

Spread each round with one
teaspoon cream cheese mixture. Top with
assorted vegetables, as desired. Add
parsley or dill sprigs just before serving.
Makes 32.

Sherried Shrimp Sandwiches
Turkey-Watercress-&-Cranberry Sandwiches
Vegetable Canapés

Checkerboard Cheese Sandwiches are the perfect snack for the cheese lovers in your crowd, while oven-fresh Cranberry-Buttermilk Scones will tempt everyone to enjoy two…or three!

Checkerboard Cheese Sandwiches

You can also serve this cheesy filling as a dip with fresh veggies and crackers.

10-oz. block extra-sharp Cheddar cheese, shredded
10-oz. block Swiss cheese, shredded
1¼ c. mayonnaise
4-oz. jar diced pimiento, drained
1 t. dried, minced onion
¼ t. pepper
20 thin white bread slices, crusts trimmed
20 thin wheat bread slices, crusts trimmed

Stir first 6 ingredients together. Spread half of mixture evenly on half of white bread slices; top with remaining half of white bread slices. Spread remaining half of mixture evenly on half of wheat bread slices; top with remaining half of wheat bread slices.

Cut each sandwich into 4 squares. Arrange, stacked in pairs, on a serving plate in a checkerboard pattern, alternating white and wheat. Makes 40.

Poppy Seed Mini Muffins

Split and top with a tiny scoop of ice cream for the children.

2 c. all-purpose flour
1 T. brown sugar, packed
1½ t. baking powder
⅛ t. salt
¼ c. butter, softened
8-oz. pkg. shredded Cheddar cheese
1 c. buttermilk
1 egg, beaten
1 T. poppy seed

Sift first 4 ingredients together. Mix in butter; stir in cheese. Add buttermilk and egg; mix just until moistened. Stir in poppy seed. Spoon into greased miniature muffin cups to ¾ full. Bake at 400 degrees for 12 to 16 minutes or until tops are golden. Makes about 3 dozen.

Donna Rasheed
Greer, SC

Lemon Tea Loaf

The lemon flavor is so refreshing with your favorite beverage.

½ c. butter, softened
¾ c. sugar
2 eggs
1 c. buttermilk
¼ t. lemon extract
2 c. all-purpose flour
½ t. baking soda
½ t. salt
2 T. frozen lemonade concentrate, thawed

Beat butter and sugar until fluffy; add eggs and beat well. Beat in buttermilk and lemon extract. Combine next 3 ingredients; stir into buttermilk mixture. Pour in a greased and floured 8"x4" loaf pan. Bake at 350 degrees for 60 to 65 minutes or until lightly golden. Remove from oven and brush lightly with lemonade concentrate; cool. Makes 6 to 8 servings.

Checkerboard Cheese Sandwiches

Cranberry-Buttermilk Scones
Homemade Devonshire Cream

Cranberry-Buttermilk Scones

*Best enjoyed warm from the oven topped
with butter or Devonshire cream.*

2 c. all-purpose flour
$1/3$ c. sugar
$1^1/2$ t. baking powder
$1/2$ t. baking soda
$1/4$ t. salt
6 T. butter, softened
$1/2$ c. buttermilk
1 egg
$1^1/2$ t. vanilla extract
$2/3$ c. sweetened, dried cranberries

Stir first 5 ingredients
together; cut in butter with a
pastry blender. Combine remaining
ingredients except cranberries;
mix into flour mixture until just
moistened. Add cranberries; drop
by $1/4$ cupfuls onto a greased baking
sheet. Bake at 375 degrees for
15 to 19 minutes or until golden.
Makes 10.

*Jenny Sisson
Broomfield, CO*

Homemade Devonshire Cream

A must for scones.

1 c. whipping cream
$1/2$ c. sour cream
2 t. powdered sugar

Beat whipping cream until soft
peaks form. Blend in sour cream
and powdered sugar. Chill and
serve. (Will keep no longer than
4 to 6 hours in refrigerator.)
Makes $2^3/4$ cups.

Tiny Pecan Tassies are a sweet indulgence your friends will adore. Why not make extras to send home with each guest? If you have a coffee urn or insulated carafe, make up a generous amount of Friendship Sip Mix ahead of time. That way, everyone can serve their own warm cups of the spicy citrus-flavored drink.

Pecan Tassies

Iced Shortbread Cookies
Buttery and rich...just like the perfect shortbread should be.

1¼ c. all-purpose flour
3 T. sugar
½ c. butter, softened

Stir together flour and sugar in a mixing bowl; cut in butter with a fork or pastry cutter. Mix until a soft dough forms. Shape cookies into walnut-size balls and place on ungreased baking sheets. Press thumb in the center of each cookie. Bake at 325 degrees for 20 to 25 minutes or until lightly golden; remove to cooling racks. Spread icing in the center of each cookie. Makes about 1½ dozen.

Icing:
¼ c. butter
2 c. powdered sugar
1 t. vanilla extract
Optional: food coloring
milk

Melt butter in a saucepan; cook over medium heat until butter is dark golden in color. Combine butter, powdered sugar and vanilla in a mixing bowl; add food coloring, if desired. Add milk, if needed, for spreading consistency.

Nancy Morris
Adams, TN

Ginger Crinkles
These tasty cookies just sparkle from being rolled in sugar.

2¼ c. all-purpose flour
2 t. baking soda
1 t. ground ginger
1 t. cinnamon
½ t. ground cloves
¼ t. salt
1 c. brown sugar, packed
¾ c. oil
¼ c. molasses
1 egg
sugar

Sift together flour, baking soda, spices and salt; set aside. In a mixing bowl, combine brown sugar, oil, molasses and egg; beat well. Add flour mixture to brown sugar mixture; stir until well blended. Shape into one-inch balls; roll in sugar. Arrange on baking sheets and bake at 375 degrees for 10 minutes. Makes 4 dozen.

Sharon Crider
Lebanon, MO

Pecan Tassies
This is a family favorite that can be made ahead.

½ c. butter or margarine, softened
3-oz. pkg. cream cheese, softened
1 c. all-purpose flour
1½ c. brown sugar, packed
2 eggs, lightly beaten
2 T. butter or margarine, melted
1 t. vanilla extract
⅔ c. chopped pecans

Beat softened butter and cream cheese at medium speed with an electric mixer until creamy. Gradually add flour, beating well. Cover and chill 2 hours.

Shape dough into 30 one-inch balls; press balls into lightly greased miniature muffin pans. Set aside.

Combine brown sugar and next 3 ingredients; stir well. Stir in pecans. Spoon 1 tablespoon pecan mixture into each pastry shell. Bake at 350 degrees for 25 minutes. Remove from pans immediately and cool completely on wire racks. Makes 2½ dozen.

Dreamy Hot Chocolate
So creamy and rich.

14-oz. can sweetened condensed
   milk
$^1/_3$ c. baking cocoa
2 t. vanilla extract
6 c. boiling water, divided
Garnishes: whipped cream,
   cinnamon

Combine condensed milk and cocoa in a saucepan; stir over low heat until smooth and warm. Add vanilla and one cup boiling water; mix well. Stir in remaining water. Top each serving with garnishes, if desired. Makes 6 to 8 servings.

Patty Fosnight
Baytown, TX

Friendship Sip Mix
This fruity drink really takes the chill off a cold winter's day.

2 c. orange drink mix
1 c. lemonade drink mix
$1^1/_3$ c. sugar
$1^1/_2$ t. cinnamon
$^1/_2$ t. ground cloves
Garnish: orange slices

Mix all ingredients together; store in an airtight container. For each serving, stir 2 tablespoons mix into one cup boiling water. Garnish, if desired. Makes 4 cups mix and 32 servings.

Friendship Sip Mix

Dainty Turkey Sandwiches
Garnish half of these finger sandwiches for the grown-ups at your party, leaving the other half plain for the little ones.

$^1/_2$ lb. smoked turkey breast, cut
   into 1-inch cubes
$^1/_2$ c. unsalted butter, cut into
   pieces and softened
1 T. orange marmalade
2 t. honey mustard
2 t. lemon juice
$^1/_4$ c. fresh parsley, chopped
3 T. fresh chives, chopped
$^1/_4$ t. salt
16 firm white bread slices
Garnishes: fresh whole chives or
   $^1/_4$ c. unsalted soft butter
   and $^1/_4$ c. fresh chopped
   parsley

Process turkey in a food processor until chopped. Add $^1/_2$ cup butter and next 3 ingredients; process until almost smooth, stopping to scrape down sides. Transfer turkey spread to a medium bowl. Stir in $^1/_4$ cup parsley, 3 tablespoons chives and salt. Trim crusts from bread, using a serrated or an electric knife.

Spread about $^1/_4$ cup turkey spread on each of 8 bread slices. Top with remaining 8 bread slices. Cut each sandwich into 4 fingers.

To garnish, tie a whole chive around each finger sandwich and knot, or spread cut sides of sandwiches with $^1/_4$ cup softened butter and dip lightly into $^1/_4$ cup chopped parsley, if desired. Arrange on a serving platter.

Note: You can make sandwiches up to one day ahead. Just lay a damp paper towel over sandwiches before covering with plastic wrap. Store in refrigerator. Makes 32.

JUST MIX IT!

For all those times when you wish you had an extra gift on hand, or when company drops by and you need a quick-fix meal or snack...homemade mixes are the answer! These seasonings and sweets are fast to finish by adding a few fresh ingredients, while the Mitten Mix for snacking is ready to serve. Package these recipes for a last-minute present, or simply keep them in your pantry for future enjoyment.

Mom's Secret Spaghetti Seasoning Mix

Mom's Secret Spaghetti Seasoning Mix

Mom's Secret Spaghetti Seasoning Mix

This mix is a quick start to a delicious meal.

1 T. dried, minced onion
1 T. cornstarch
1 T. dried parsley
2 t. green pepper flakes
1½ t. salt
1 t. sugar
1 t. dried oregano
¾ t. Italian seasonings
¼ t. dried, minced garlic

Combine all ingredients; store in an airtight container. Makes about ⅓ cup.

To serve: Brown one pound ground beef; drain. Add two, 8-oz. cans tomato sauce, a 6-oz. can tomato paste, 2¾ cups tomato juice or water and seasoning mix to the beef; simmer sauce 30 minutes, stirring occasionally. Serve over prepared spaghetti. Makes 4 to 6 servings.

Vickie

CHRISTMAS IS FOR SHARING

Mitten Mix

Mitten Mix

This is one snack mix no one gets tired of eating!

6 T. butter, melted
2 T. Worcestershire sauce
1½ t. seasoned salt
¾ t. garlic powder
½ t. onion powder
3 c. bite-size crispy corn cereal
   squares
3 c. bite-size crispy rice cereal
   squares
3 c. bite-size crispy wheat cereal
   squares
1 c. mixed nuts
1 c. pretzels
1 c. garlic-flavored bagel chips

Whisk first 5 ingredients together; set aside. Toss remaining ingredients together in a roasting pan; pour butter mixture over the top. Mix gently until cereal, nuts, pretzels and bagel chips are coated; bake at 325 degrees for 45 minutes, stirring every 10 minutes. Makes 3 quarts.

Rebekah Neal
Springdale, AR

Always convenient, mixes make thoughtful gifts. Try putting Mitten Mix in plastic bags to tuck into mittens for a quick gift. The dry ingredients for Warm-'Em-Up Alphabet Soup Mix can be layered in quart jars for a pretty presentation.

Tasty Taco Seasoning Mix

Use this mix to flavor beef, chicken, soups, meatballs and refried beans.

¾ c. dried, minced onion
¼ c. salt
¼ c. chili powder
2 T. cumin
2 T. cornstarch
2 T. red pepper flakes
1 T. dried oregano
1 T. garlic powder
1 T. onion salt

Combine ingredients in a large plastic zipping bag; close tightly. Shake to mix well. Makes 2 cups.

To serve: Add 2 tablespoons mix to one pound browned ground beef and ½ cup water; heat through. Serves 4.

Bacon Dip Spice Packet

Seal the mix in a small plastic zipping bag and label for a quick & easy dip mix packet.

2 T. bacon bits
1 T. dried, minced onion
1 t. beef bouillon granules
⅛ t. dried, minced garlic
⅛ t. dried chives

Combine all ingredients; mix well. Place in an airtight container. Makes about ¼ cup.

To serve: Whisk one cup sour cream and spice mix together; cover and refrigerate for at least one hour before serving. Makes one cup.

Bowl o' Bruschetta Blend

Just like the kind at the family-style Italian restaurants.

1-lb. pkg. Roma tomatoes, chopped and seeded
1/3 c. sweet onion, diced
1/4 c. olive oil
1/4 c. garlic, minced
2 T. fresh basil, chopped
1/4 t. salt
1/4 t. pepper

Combine all ingredients in a large mixing bowl; whisk well. Pour into an airtight container and refrigerate until ready to serve. Makes 2 to 3 cups.

To serve: Slice one loaf round bread in half horizontally so there are 2, one-inch thick bread circles; cut each into 5 wedges. Brush with garlic-olive oil; broil until golden. Place on a serving dish; spoon bruschetta blend on top. Makes 10 servings.

Snappy BBQ Seasoning Mix

Keep this mix on hand for a quick way to add extra spice to your food!

3 T. onion powder
3 T. garlic powder
2 T. dried parsley
2 T. celery salt
2 T. dry mustard
1 T. pepper

Blend all ingredients together and store in an airtight container. When ready to use, sprinkle on beef, pork or fish while grilling or broiling. Makes about 3/4 cup.

*Lynda Short
Janesville, WI*

Warm-'Em-Up Alphabet Soup Mix

A fun soup for kids just learning their ABC's!

1/2 c. pearled barley
1/2 c. dried split peas
1/2 c. instant rice, uncooked
1/2 c. dried lentils
2 T. dried, minced onion
2 T. dried parsley
2 1/2 t. salt
1/2 t. lemon pepper
2 T. beef bouillon granules
1/2 c. alphabet pasta, uncooked
1 c. rotini, uncooked

In a one-quart, wide-mouth jar, layer the ingredients in the order listed. Seal the lid. Makes one quart.

To serve: Add all ingredients to 3 quarts water in a large pot. Add 2 stalks chopped celery, 2 sliced carrots, one cup shredded cabbage and 2 cups diced tomatoes. Cover and cook over medium-low heat for one hour or until vegetables are tender. Makes 10 to 12 servings.

Warm-'Em-Up Alphabet Soup Mix

Home-Sweet-Home Stroganoff Mix

Need a quick meal? Just add this mix to cooked beef and serve over noodles...yum!

2 c. powdered milk
1 c. cornstarch
1/4 c. chicken bouillon granules
3 T. dried, minced onion
2 T. dried parsley
1 T. garlic powder
1 t. dried basil
1 t. dried thyme
1 t. pepper

Combine all ingredients; place in an airtight jar or plastic zipping bag. Makes about 3³/₄ cups.

To serve: Brown one pound ground beef in a 12" skillet; drain. Add 2 cups water, 2 cups uncooked egg noodles and 1/2 cup stroganoff mix; stir to combine. Bring to a boil; reduce heat and simmer, covered, for 15 to 20 minutes. Top with 1/2 cup sour cream or plain yogurt; serve warm. Makes 4 servings.

For those times when a snack attack has you searching the kitchen, Blonde Brownie Mix and Peanut Butter Cup Cookie Mix come to your rescue. They're also sweet gifts for households with kids!

Blonde Brownie Mix

Here's a mix that the kids can do themselves!

16-oz. pkg. brown sugar
2 c. all-purpose flour
1/2 c. chopped pecans

Combine all ingredients in a heavy-duty plastic zipping bag. Makes about 5 cups.

To bake: Combine brownie mix with 4 eggs; stir well. Pour into a greased 13"x9" pan. Bake at 350 degrees for 25 to 30 minutes. Makes 2 dozen.

Kathy Grashoff
Ft. Wayne, IN

Relaxing Tea Creamer Mix

Stirred into tea, this mix creates a delightful Chai-like drink...add 1/4 teaspoon white pepper for even more spice.

14-oz. can sweetened condensed
    milk
1 t. cardamom
1 t. sugar
3/4 t. cinnamon
1/2 t. ground cloves
1/2 t. nutmeg

Stir all ingredients together; cover and refrigerate for at least 24 hours. Pour into an airtight container. Store in refrigerator. Makes about 2 cups.

To serve: Add 2 teaspoons creamer to a cup of strongly brewed black tea; stir well. Makes one serving.

Blonde Brownie Mix

Peanut Butter Cup Cookie Mix

Peanut Butter Cup Cookie Mix

Peanut butter lovers won't be able to resist.

20 mini peanut butter cups, chopped
1³/₄ c. all-purpose flour
³/₄ c. sugar
¹/₂ c. brown sugar, packed
1 t. baking powder
¹/₂ t. baking soda

Place peanut butter cups in a plastic zipping bag. Combine remaining ingredients in another plastic zipping bag. Makes about 3 cups dry mix.

To bake: Place dry mix in a large bowl. Add ¹/₂ cup softened butter, one slightly beaten egg and one teaspoon vanilla extract; stir until completely blended (mixture will be crumbly). Stir in peanut butter cups. Shape dough into 1¹/₂-inch balls and place on greased baking sheets. Bake at 375 degrees for 12 to 14 minutes; cool 5 minutes before removing cookies to wire racks to cool completely. Makes 2 dozen.

simply wonderful

To help you during the busy holiday season, the Country Friends gathered these flavor-packed recipes that are quick & easy to make. Kate uses refrigerated ravioli to prepare Pasta with Tomato-Basil Cream. Holly's favorite is Chicken and Rice Casserole, a hearty dish that takes less time to prepare when you use a deli-roasted chicken. A couple of these recipes also make an extra dish for the freezer...Mary Elizabeth likes to keep a pan of Smoked Turkey Tetrazzini on hand for a quick food gift.

Pasta with Tomato-Basil Cream

So simple, but so good!

20-oz. pkg. refrigerated four-cheese ravioli
16-oz. jar sun-dried tomato Alfredo sauce
2 T. white wine or water
14.5-oz. can chopped tomatoes, well drained
1/2 c. fresh basil, chopped
1/3 c. shredded Parmesan cheese
Garnishes: fresh basil strips, shredded Parmesan
   cheese

Prepare pasta according to package directions; set aside. Pour Alfredo sauce into a medium saucepan. Pour wine or water into sauce jar. Cover tightly and shake well; stir into saucepan. Stir in tomatoes, 1/2 cup chopped basil and 1/3 cup shredded Parmesan cheese. Cook over medium-low heat 5 minutes or until thoroughly heated; toss with pasta. Garnish, if desired. Makes 4 to 6 servings.

Chicken and Rice Casserole

If you are in a hurry, use meat from a deli-roasted chicken.

6.2-oz. pkg. fast-cooking long-grain and wild rice mix
2 T. butter
1 onion, chopped
2 stalks celery, chopped
3 c. cooked chicken, chopped
3 c. shredded Colby-Jack cheese blend, divided
$10^3/_4$-oz. can cream of mushroom soup
1 c. sour cream
$^1/_2$ c. milk
$^1/_2$ t. salt
$^1/_2$ t. pepper
1 c. round buttery crackers, crushed

Prepare rice mix according to package directions; set aside. Melt butter in a large skillet over medium-high heat; add onion and celery. Sauté 4 minutes or until tender.

Combine rice, sautéed vegetables, chicken, 2 cups cheese and next 5 ingredients; spoon into a lightly greased 5-quart slow cooker. Cover and cook on low setting $4^1/_2$ hours.

Combine remaining one cup cheese and cracker crumbs; sprinkle over casserole. Cover and cook on low setting 30 more minutes. Makes 6 servings.

Chicken-and-Black Bean Enchiladas

Even if you stop at the store for these ingredients, dinner will be ready in no time at all.

whole deli-roasted chicken (about 3 cups), chopped
15-oz. can black beans, rinsed and drained
10-oz. can diced tomatoes with green chiles
$8^3/_4$-oz. can no-salt-added corn, drained
8-oz. pkg. shredded Mexican four-cheese blend, divided
8 8-inch whole wheat flour tortillas
non-stick vegetable spray
2 10-oz. cans enchilada sauce
Garnishes: chopped tomatoes, onions and cilantro

Combine first 4 ingredients and $1^1/_2$ cups cheese in a large bowl. Spoon chicken mixture evenly down the center of each tortilla and roll up. Arrange, seam side down, in a 13"x9" baking dish coated with vegetable spray. Pour enchilada sauce evenly over tortillas and sprinkle evenly with remaining $^1/_2$ cup cheese. Bake, covered, at 350 degrees for 20 minutes. Remove foil and bake 15 more minutes or until bubbly. Garnish, if desired. Makes 8 servings.

Chicken-and-Black Bean Enchiladas

When dishes are this simple to whip up, you can get out of the kitchen quick! Because you use a cooked chicken from the deli, Chicken-and-Black Bean Enchiladas almost prepare themselves. Make Simple Meatloaf ahead of time, so you can make Italian Meatloaf Sandwiches in just minutes.

Simple Meatloaf

Make two recipes and freeze one for Italian Meatloaf Sandwiches.

1½ lbs. ground beef
¾ c. quick-cooking oats, uncooked
½ c. milk
¼ c. onion, chopped
1 egg, lightly beaten
1 t. salt
¼ t. pepper
⅓ c. ketchup
2 T. brown sugar, packed
1 T. yellow mustard

Combine first 7 ingredients in a large bowl just until blended; place in a lightly greased 8"x4" loaf pan. Stir together ketchup, brown sugar and mustard; pour evenly over meatloaf. Bake at 350 degrees for one hour. Remove from oven; let stand 5 minutes and remove from pan before slicing. Makes 6 servings.

To freeze: Wrap meatloaf in plastic wrap and aluminum foil; freeze up to one month. Thaw in refrigerator.

Italian Meatloaf Sandwich

Italian Meatloaf Sandwiches

This great flavor combo also works with leftover roast beef or pot roast.

14-oz. French bread loaf
4 one-inch-thick cold meatloaf slices
1 c. marinara or spaghetti sauce
8-oz. pkg. shredded Italian cheese blend
¼ t. dried Italian seasoning

Cut bread into fourths; cut quarters in half horizontally. Place bread quarters, cut sides up, on a baking sheet. Top each bread bottom with one meatloaf slice, 2 tablespoons marinara sauce and ¼ cup cheese. Top each bread top with 2 tablespoons marinara sauce and ¼ cup cheese; sprinkle with Italian seasoning.

Bake at 375 degrees for 10 to 15 minutes or until cheese melts and meat is thoroughly heated. Top bread bottoms with bread tops and serve sandwiches immediately. Makes 4 servings.

Beef Burgundy Stew

Two more wonderful ways to cut your kitchen time in half...Beef Burgundy Stew can simmer in a slow cooker, or you can layer a Shepherd's Pie with fully cooked beef and veggies from the freezer!

Beef Burgundy Stew

This classic recipe works well in a slow cooker.

6 bacon slices, chopped
2 lbs. beef stew meat
16-oz. pkg. frozen pearl onions, thawed
8-oz. pkg. mushrooms, quartered
6 red potatoes, quartered
2 carrots, cut into $\frac{1}{2}$-inch pieces
14-oz. can beef broth
1 c. Burgundy, dry red wine or beef broth
2 T. tomato paste
1 T. fresh thyme leaves
1 t. salt
$\frac{1}{4}$ t. pepper
3 cloves garlic, minced
2 T. cornstarch
2 t. cold water

Cook bacon in a large skillet over medium-high heat until crisp. Remove bacon, reserving drippings in pan. Set bacon aside.

Brown beef, in batches, in reserved bacon drippings until browned on all sides. Combine reserved bacon, beef, onions and next 10 ingredients in a 5-quart slow cooker. Cover and cook on low setting 7 hours or until beef and vegetables are tender. Whisk together cornstarch and water. Stir into stew. Cover and cook on high setting one hour or until slightly thickened. Makes 9 cups.

Foolproof Pot Roast

Fast, easy and tasty...what a great combination!

16-oz. pkg. fully cooked beef pot roast in gravy
non-stick vegetable spray
1 onion, thinly sliced
1 T. butter
1 t. balsamic vinegar
$\frac{1}{2}$ t. sugar
$\frac{1}{4}$ t. salt
$\frac{1}{4}$ t. pepper

Heat roast according to package directions. Remove roast from package, reserving liquid. Let stand 2 minutes. Cut into 8 pieces.

Coat a large non-stick skillet with non-stick vegetable spray; place over medium-high heat until hot. Add onion and sauté 10 minutes or until browned.

Add reserved liquid, roast, butter and remaining ingredients to pan. Stir well and bring to a boil. Boil 30 seconds or until thoroughly heated. Makes 4 servings.

Shepherd's Pie

Thanks to purchased pre-made ingredients, new cooks can get that "made from scatch" taste.

2 17-oz. pkgs. fully cooked beef tips with gravy
1 c. frozen whole kernel corn, thawed
1 c. frozen sweet peas, thawed
24-oz. pkg. refrigerated mashed potatoes
1/2 of an 8-oz. pkg. cream cheese, softened
1 T. butter or margarine, softened
1 t. garlic powder
1 c. shredded sharp Cheddar cheese

Cook beef according to package directions. Spoon beef into a lightly greased 11"x7" baking dish. Top with corn and peas; set aside.

Cook potatoes according to package directions; spoon potatoes into a bowl. Add cream cheese, butter and garlic powder; beat at medium speed with an electric mixer until smooth. Spread potato mixture over vegetables; sprinkle with cheese.

Bake, uncovered, at 350 degrees for 15 minutes or until thoroughly heated. Makes 8 servings.

Smoked Turkey Tetrazzini

Two meals taken care of with one preparation time.

12 oz. vermicelli, broken in half
1 T. butter or margarine
1 onion, chopped
8-oz. pkg. sliced mushrooms
1 t. bottled minced garlic
4 c. cubed smoked or honey-roasted turkey (about 1 1/2 lbs.)
1 1/4 c. shredded Cheddar cheese, divided
1/4 c. grated Parmesan cheese
10 3/4-oz. can cream of mushroom soup
10 3/4-oz. can cream of celery soup
1 c. sour cream
1/2 c. chicken broth
1/2 t. salt
1/2 t. pepper

Cook vermicelli according to package directions; set aside. Melt butter in a Dutch oven over medium-high heat. Add onion, mushrooms and garlic; sauté 5 minutes or until tender. Stir in turkey, 3/4 cup Cheddar cheese and remaining 7 ingredients.

Drain vermicelli and add to turkey mixture; stir well.

Spoon mixture into 2 lightly greased 8"x8" baking dishes; sprinkle with remaining 1/2 cup Cheddar cheese. Cover each casserole tightly in aluminum foil; freeze up to 2 months.

Remove desired number of casseroles from freezer, leaving foil intact. Bake at 350 degrees for 2 hours; uncover and bake 15 more minutes or until bubbly. Each casserole makes 8 servings.

To bake without freezing: Prepare recipe omitting the covering and freezing process. Bake, uncovered, at 350 degrees for 30 minutes or until bubbly.

To thaw and bake: Let desired number of casseroles thaw overnight in refrigerator. Leave foil cover intact and bake at 350 degrees for one hour and 15 minutes. Uncover and bake 15 more minutes or until bubbly.

Shepherd's Pie

Delightful Desserts

If you think dessert should always taste as good as it looks, then you'll find plenty to love about this recipe collection! Chocolate is the theme for the tempting Cookie Dough Cheesecake, Rocky Road Treats and Dreamy Chocolate Peppermints. For cinnamon lovers, Rich Spice Cake and Cookie Jar Gingersnaps are sure to become new favorites. Remember, it's always better to make extras at Christmastime!

Cookie Dough Cheesecake

Who can resist cookie dough? Indulge in this!

1³/₄ c. chocolate chip cookie crumbs
1¹/₂ c. sugar, divided
¹/₂ c. butter, melted and divided
3 8-oz. pkgs. cream cheese, softened
3 eggs
1 c. sour cream
1¹/₂ t. vanilla extract, divided
¹/₄ c. brown sugar, packed
¹/₂ c. all-purpose flour
1¹/₂ c. mini semi-sweet chocolate chips, divided

In a small bowl, combine cookie crumbs and ¹/₄ cup sugar; stir in ¹/₄ cup butter. Press into bottom and slightly up the sides of a greased 9" springform pan; set aside.

In a mixing bowl, beat cream cheese and one cup sugar until smooth. Add eggs; beat on low speed just until combined. Add sour cream and ¹/₂ teaspoon vanilla; beat just until blended. Pour over crust; set aside.

In a separate mixing bowl, beat remaining ¹/₄ cup butter, remaining ¹/₄ cup sugar and brown sugar on medium speed; add remaining one teaspoon vanilla. Gradually add flour and stir in one cup chocolate chips. Drop by teaspoonfuls over filling, gently pushing dough below surface. Bake at 350 degrees for 50 to 55 minutes or until center is almost set. Cool on a wire rack for 10 minutes. Carefully run a knife around the edge of pan to loosen; cool one hour longer. Refrigerate overnight, then remove sides of pan and sprinkle with remaining ¹/₂ cup chips. Makes 8 servings.

Valarie Dobbins
Edmond, OK

When company shows up, treat them to their choice of these oh-so-good desserts. Chocolate, spices and peanut butter are all such welcome Christmas flavors!

Rocky Road Treats

Rocky Road Treats

If you love rocky road ice cream, try these chocolatey squares.

1/2 c. butter, melted
1 c. sugar
1/3 c. baking cocoa
2 eggs
2 t. vanilla extract
1 c. all-purpose flour
1/2 t. baking powder
2/3 c. chopped pecans, divided
1/3 c. toffee bits

Whisk butter, sugar, cocoa, eggs and vanilla together; add flour and baking powder. Fold in 1/3 cup pecans; spread in a greased aluminum foil-lined 9"x9" baking pan. Bake at 350 degrees for 20 minutes; cool. Pour icing over the top. Sprinkle with remaining 1/3 cup pecans and toffee bits. Cool and cut into bars. Makes 20.

Marshmallow Icing:
1 c. mini marshmallows
1/2 c. powdered sugar
3 T. butter
2 T. baking cocoa
2 T. milk

Combine all ingredients in a heavy saucepan; heat over medium-low heat. Stir until marshmallows melt and mixture is smooth.

Tina Wright
Atlanta, GA

Rich Spice Cake

Rich Spice Cake

A family favorite from one of my Grandmother's oldest cookbooks dated 1928.

2 c. plus 1 T. all-purpose flour, divided
2 t. cinnamon
1 t. ground cloves
1 t. allspice
1/2 t. nutmeg
1 t. baking soda
1 c. milk
2 T. vinegar
1/2 c. shortening
2 c. brown sugar, packed
3 egg yolks
2 egg whites, stiffly beaten
1 c. raisins

Sift 2 cups flour, cinnamon, cloves, allspice, nutmeg and baking soda together; set aside. Stir milk and vinegar together; set aside. Beat shortening, brown sugar and egg yolks together in a large mixing bowl. Gradually beat in flour mixture alternately with milk; fold in egg whites. Toss raisins with remaining one tablespoon flour; fold into batter. Pour into 2 greased and floured 8" round baking pans; bake at 350 degrees for 28 minutes or until a toothpick inserted into center comes out clean. Cool; frost with caramel icing. Makes 8 to 12 servings.

Caramel Icing:
3 c. brown sugar, packed
1 1/2 c. whipping cream
1 1/2 T. butter
1 1/2 t. vanilla extract

Heat brown sugar and cream together in a heavy saucepan until soft-ball stage or 234 degrees on a candy thermometer. Stir in butter and vanilla; remove from heat. Stir until desired spreading consistency is reached.

Naomi Cycak
Ligonier, PA

Peanut Butter Strudel Pie

Peanut Butter Strudel Pie

The best peanut butter pie! Topped with meringue, it's wonderful!

3/4 c. powdered sugar
1/4 c. creamy peanut butter
9-inch pie crust
2/3 c. plus 6 T. sugar, divided
1/3 c. all-purpose flour
1/4 t. salt
2 c. milk
3 eggs
2 T. butter
1/2 t. vanilla extract
1/4 t. cream of tartar

In a small bowl, combine powdered sugar and peanut butter to resemble coarse crumbs. Spread over bottom of baked pie crust, reserving one tablespoon for topping.

In a 2-quart saucepan, stir together 2/3 cup sugar, flour and salt; gradually add milk. Bring mixture to a boil over medium heat, stirring constantly; cook and stir 5 minutes or until thickened. Remove from heat and set aside.

Separate eggs, placing whites in a separate bowl. Beat egg yolks and blend in a small amount of milk mixture; stir well. Return to pan; cook and stir over low heat for 3 minutes. Remove from heat and stir in butter and vanilla. Cover and set filling aside.

Beat egg whites and cream of tartar until foamy. Gradually beat in remaining 6 tablespoons sugar, one tablespoon at a time, beating until stiff peaks form.

Reheat filling over medium heat, stirring constantly, just until hot. Pour hot filling over peanut butter crumbs in pie crust. Spread meringue over pie, being sure to touch edges of crust to seal. Sprinkle remaining one tablespoon peanut butter crumbs over meringue. Bake at 325 degrees for 25 minutes or until meringue is golden. Cool completely before serving. Makes 6 to 8 servings.

Phyllis Laughrey
Mt. Vernon, OH

Vermont Maple Cookies

More treats for guests…or for the family while you trim the tree. Cookies, candy and creamy fondue are sweet delights for wintry nights!

Vermont Maple Cookies
It's the maple-butter glaze that makes these cookies so good.

1/2 c. shortening
1 c. brown sugar, packed
1/2 c. sugar
2 eggs
1 c. sour cream
1 T. maple flavoring
2 3/4 c. all-purpose flour
1 t. salt
1/2 t. baking soda
1 c. chopped walnuts

Combine shortening, sugars and eggs thoroughly; stir in sour cream and maple flavoring. In a separate bowl, mix flour, salt and baking soda together; blend into sugar mixture. Stir in walnuts and drop by rounded tablespoonfuls, about 2 inches apart, onto a greased baking sheet. Bake at 375 degrees for about 10 minutes or until almost no imprint shows when lightly touched. Cool; ice with glaze. Makes about 4 dozen.

Maple-Butter Glaze:
1/2 c. butter
2 c. powdered sugar
2 t. maple flavoring
3 T. hot water

Heat butter until golden brown; mix in powdered sugar and maple flavoring. Stir in water gradually until glaze is smooth.

Pam Wagner
Ford City, PA

Dreamy Chocolate Peppermints
I always get requests for these…one taste and you'll know why!

16-oz. pkg. powdered sugar
2 T. butter, softened
2 1/2 t. peppermint extract
1/2 t. vanilla extract
1/4 c. evaporated milk
12-oz. pkg. semi-sweet chocolate chips
2 T. shortening

Combine powdered sugar, butter and extracts. Add evaporated milk, mixing well. Roll into one-inch balls and place on wax paper-lined baking sheets; chill 30 minutes.

Flatten each round to 1/4-inch thickness with the bottom of a smooth glass; chill 45 minutes.

In a double boiler, melt chocolate chips and shortening, stirring often. Remove from heat. Working quickly, dip patties into chocolate; place back on wax paper and chill until chocolate hardens. Makes 3 to 4 dozen.

Kathy Boswell
Virginia Beach, VA

Cookie Jar Gingersnaps
These spicy cookies taste wonderful. They're great for a holiday open house or cookie exchange.

2 c. all-purpose flour
1 T. ground ginger
2 t. baking soda
1 t. cinnamon
1/2 t. salt
3/4 c. shortening
2 c. sugar, divided
1 egg
1/4 c. molasses

Sift together flour, ginger, baking soda, cinnamon and salt. Beat shortening and one cup sugar until well blended. Beat in egg and molasses. Mix in dry ingredients; form into small balls and roll in remaining one cup sugar. Place 2 inches apart on an ungreased baking sheet. Bake at 350 degrees from 12 to 15 minutes or until tops are rounded, crackly and golden. Makes about 4 dozen.

Susan Kennedy
Delaware, OH

Ooey-Gooey Fondue-y

Anything you dip in this chocolate will taste wonderful!

14-oz. can condensed milk
6-oz. pkg. butterscotch chips
4 1-oz. sqs. unsweetened baking
    chocolate
7-oz. jar marshmallow creme
1/2 c. milk
1 t. vanilla extract

Combine all ingredients in a saucepan; heat over low heat until melted and smooth, stirring often. Pour into a fondue pot or a 2-quart slow cooker; keep warm over low heat. Makes 3 1/2 cups.

Cors Burns
Delaware, OH

Ooey-Gooey Fondue-y

White Confetti Fudge

I like to keep this on hand...just to snack on.

1 1/2 lbs. white baking chocolate
14-oz. can sweetened
    condensed milk
1/2 c. red candied cherries,
    chopped
1/2 c. green candied cherries,
    chopped
1 t. vanilla extract
1/8 t. salt

Melt chocolate with milk in a heavy saucepan; stir constantly. Remove from heat; stir in remaining ingredients. Spread evenly in a buttered aluminum foil-lined 8"x8" baking pan; chill about 2 hours or until firm.

Use foil to lift fudge from pan onto a cutting board; remove foil and cut into small squares. Makes 2 dozen.

Angela Nichols
Mt. Airy, NC

Christmas
Vacation
Dec. 22

MRS. STEWART

Food for Friends

Often, the best gifts of Christmas for your family & friends are home-cooked meals or fresh baked goods! Why not let your neighbors know you're thinking of them with Pot Roast & Dumplings, or take a batch of Caramel Apple Muffins to a favorite teacher? We've included some main-course dishes that freeze and reheat well. These make-ahead meals are also terrific for your family during the holiday season!

Farmgirl Chocolate Chippers

Farmgirl Chocolate Chippers

A great recipe when you need a lot of cookies!

2 c. butter, softened
2 c. sugar
2 c. brown sugar, packed
4 eggs, beaten
2 t. vanilla extract
5 c. long-cooking oats, uncooked
4 c. all-purpose flour
2 t. baking powder
2 t. baking soda
1 t. salt
2 12-oz. pkgs. semi-sweet chocolate chips
7-oz. pkg. chocolate candy bar, grated
3 c. chopped pecans

Blend together butter, sugar and brown sugar in a large bowl; mix well. Add eggs and vanilla; set aside.

Working in batches, process oats in a blender or food processor until powdery. Combine oats, flour, baking powder, baking soda and salt in a large bowl; mix into butter mixture. Stir in chocolate chips, grated chocolate and pecans. Form into 2-inch balls; arrange on ungreased baking sheets 2 inches apart. Bake at 375 degrees for 6 minutes. Makes 10 dozen.

Mary Murray
Gooseberry Patch

Who wouldn't love a gift of Lisa's Best-Ever Lasagna or savory Country Chicken Pot Pies? Both entrées are freezer-friendly and so good to have on hand!

Lisa's Best-Ever Lasagna

If you can assemble this the day before, it's even better.

2 24-oz. jars spaghetti sauce
14½-oz. can diced tomatoes, drained
10¾-oz. can tomato purée
2 3.8-oz. cans sliced black olives, drained
1 onion, diced
1 red pepper, chopped
1 yellow pepper, chopped
¼ c. sugar
1 clove garlic, minced
1 t. dried oregano
24 oz. shredded mozzarella cheese
12 oz. shredded Monterey Jack cheese
8 oz. provolone cheese, shredded
1 c. grated Parmesan cheese
non-stick vegetable spray
16-oz. pkg. lasagna noodles, cooked

Combine first 10 ingredients in a large stockpot over medium heat. Simmer for one hour. Mix together cheeses; set aside. Spray two 13"x9" baking pans with non-stick vegetable spray. Spread a thin layer of sauce mixture in pans. Layer lasagna noodles, sauce and cheese. Repeat layers for a total of 3 layers. Bake at 350 degrees for 30 to 40 minutes or until golden and bubbly. Each casserole makes 8 to 10 servings.

Lisa Hill
Salinas, CA

Lisa's Best-Ever Lasagna

Country Chicken Pot Pies

Caramel Apple Muffins

An extra-special breakfast treat.

2 c. all-purpose flour
³/₄ c. sugar
2¹/₂ t. cinnamon
2 t. baking powder
¹/₂ t. salt
1 c. milk
¹/₄ c. butter, melted
1 egg, beaten
1¹/₂ t. vanilla extract
¹/₂ c. apple, cored, peeled and
    finely diced
12 caramels, unwrapped and diced

Combine flour, sugar, cinnamon, baking powder and salt in a large bowl; set aside.

In a separate large bowl, mix together milk, butter, egg and vanilla; add flour mixture, stirring just until blended. Stir in apples and caramels. Divide batter evenly in 12 paper-lined muffin cups; bake at 350 degrees for 25 minutes or until tops spring back when lightly pressed. Serve warm. Makes one dozen.

Stephanie White
Idabel, OK

Caramel Apple Muffins

Country Chicken Pot Pies

Just the perfect single serving size.

1 c. onion, chopped
1 c. celery, chopped
1 c. carrot, chopped
¹/₃ c. butter or margarine
¹/₂ c. all-purpose flour
2 c. chicken broth
1 c. half-and-half
4 c. cooked chicken, chopped
1 c. frozen peas, thawed
1 t. salt
¹/₄ t. pepper
1 egg, beaten

Sauté first 3 ingredients in butter in a skillet until tender. Add flour; stir until smooth. Cook one minute, stirring constantly. Add chicken broth and half-and-half; cook, stirring constantly, until thickened and bubbly. Stir in chicken, peas, salt and pepper.

Divide basic pastry into 8 equal portions. Roll 4 portions of pastry into 10-inch circles on a floured surface. Place in four 6-inch ceramic pie plates. Divide chicken mixture evenly over pastries in pie plates. Roll remaining 4 portions of pastry into 7-inch circles on a floured surface. Place pastry circles over filling; fold edges under and flute. Cut slits in tops to allow steam to escape. Brush with beaten egg. Bake at 400 degrees for 35 to 40 minutes or until crust is golden. Makes 4 servings.

To store: Tightly cover and freeze unbaked pies up to one month. Let stand at room temperature 30 minutes. Bake, uncovered, at 400 degrees for one hour or until crust is golden.

Basic Pastry:
4 c. all-purpose flour
2 t. salt
1¹/₂ c. plus 1 T. shortening
¹/₃ to ¹/₂ c. cold water

Combine flour and salt; cut in shortening with a pastry blender until mixture resembles coarse meal. Sprinkle cold water, one tablespoon at a time, over surface; stir with a fork until dry ingredients are moistened.

Along with all the fun of gift wrapping, stocking stuffing and cookie baking, Christmas is the perfect time of year to deliver a homemade dinner to friends or neighbors!

Slow-Cooker Taco Soup

This soup freezes well and makes enough to share with several friends.

1 lb. ground beef
1 onion, diced
1 clove garlic, minced
2 15-oz. cans black beans,
    drained and rinsed
2 c. water
15¼-oz. can corn, drained
15-oz. can tomato sauce
12-oz. bottle green taco sauce
4½-oz. can chopped green chiles
1-oz. pkg. taco seasoning mix
Garnishes: sour cream, shredded
    Cheddar cheese

Brown beef, onion and garlic in a large skillet over medium heat; drain. In a slow cooker, combine beef mixture and remaining ingredients except garnishes. Cover and cook on high setting for one hour. Garnish, if desired. Serve with corn chips. Makes 8 to 10 servings.

Susan Ahlstrand
Post Falls, ID

Slow-Cooker Taco Soup

Pot Roast & Dumplings

This is one of our favorite meals on a cold winter day. If you cook the roast overnight, you can make the dumplings the next morning. At the end of a busy day, dinner is practically ready!

2 c. baby carrots
5 potatoes, peeled and halved
4-lb. beef chuck roast
garlic salt and pepper to taste
2 c. water
1-oz. pkg. onion soup mix

Arrange carrots and potatoes in a slow cooker. Place roast on top; sprinkle with garlic salt and pepper. In a small bowl, stir together water and soup mix; pour over roast. Cover and cook on low setting for 6 to 8 hours.

Drain most of broth from slow cooker into a large soup pot; keep roast and vegetables warm in slow cooker. Bring broth to a boil over medium-high heat. Drop dumpling batter into boiling broth by teaspoonfuls. Cover and cook for 15 minutes. Serve dumplings with sliced roast and vegetables. Makes 8 to 10 servings.

Dumplings:
2 c. all-purpose flour
3 T. baking powder
$^1/_2$ t. salt
1 c. half-and-half

Stir together dry ingredients. Add half-and-half and stir quickly to make a medium-soft batter.

Wendy Sensing
Franklin, TN

Black Bottom Cupcakes

Black Bottom Cupcakes

Chocolate and cream cheese...what a scrumptious combination!

2 8-oz. pkgs. cream cheese, softened
2 eggs, beaten
$2^2/_3$ c. sugar, divided
$1^1/_4$ t. salt, divided
$1^1/_2$ c. semi-sweet chocolate chips
3 c. all-purpose flour
$^1/_2$ c. baking cocoa
2 t. baking soda
2 c. water
$^2/_3$ c. oil
2 T. vinegar
2 t. vanilla extract

Combine cream cheese, eggs, $^2/_3$ cup sugar, $^1/_4$ teaspoon salt and chocolate chips; mix well and set aside.

Combine remaining 2 cups sugar, remainng one teaspoon salt and last 7 ingredients in a large bowl; fill paper-lined muffin cups $^3/_4$ full with chocolate batter. Top each with $^1/_4$ cup cream cheese mixture. Bake at 350 degrees for 25 or 30 minutes. Makes 2 dozen.

Gretchen Brown
Forest Grove, OR

Dapper Doorman

(also shown on page 9)

- party balloons (inflated to 9" dia. for the head, two 12" elongated for the arms and four 33" elongated for the body)
- masking tape
- foam brush
- matte decoupage glue
- newspaper
- serrated knife
- white spray primer
- pink, red, black and white acrylic paints
- paintbrushes
- clear acrylic spray sealer
- mica flakes
- 2" dia. foam ball, cut in half for the nose
- air-drying clay (we used Creative Paperclay®)
- hot glue gun
- 14" dia. wooden charger
- drill with $^3/_8$" bit
- two 22" lengths of $^3/_8$" dia. dowel
- two $^3/_4$" dia. black snaps for eyes
- five $^3/_8$" dia. black snaps for mouth
- felt hat
- scarf
- medium-gauge wire
- wire cutters
- mini tinsel tree
- child's snow shovel

Keep this warm-hearted snowman on a covered porch for protection from snow or rain. Use decoupage glue for all gluing unless otherwise noted. Use primer and sealer in a well-ventilated area and allow to dry after each application.

1. Tape the 4 body balloons together (Fig. 1). To papier-mâché the body, brush glue on both sides of torn newspaper strips; overlapping the edges, cover all but the bottom end of the body with the strips. Allow to dry; then, apply one or 2 more layers. Let dry completely.

2. To add the head, cut away a 6" diameter hole at the top of the body. Tape the head balloon in place and cover the head with papier-mâché, overlapping strips onto the body to join at the neck (Fig. 2). Add papier-mâché arms in the same manner, positioning each arm as desired and joining to the body at the shoulder (Fig. 3). Allow to dry; then, apply one or 2 more layers to the head and arms.

3. When completely dry, trim the bottom edge of the snowman with the knife. Prime the snowman; then, paint the cheeks pink. Spray with several coats of sealer and while the last coat is still wet, sprinkle with mica flakes. Shake the excess onto newspaper.

4. Follow manufacturer's instructions to cover the foam nose with clay; allow to dry. Paint, then seal the nose. Hot glue the nose to the snowman.

5. For the base, paint the charger black; apply sealer. Invert the charger and drill 2 holes near the center, 4" apart. Insert the dowels. Brush a little glue on the charger and sprinkle with mica flakes. Place the snowman over the dowels.

Fig. 1   Fig. 2   Fig. 3

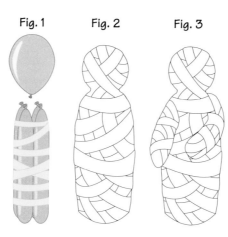

6. Glue on the snap eyes and mouth. Add the hat and scarf (we brushed a little white paint on the hat and while wet, sprinkled it with mica flakes). Wire the tree to one arm and prop the shovel against the other.

Snowman Trio

(also shown on page 10)

- serrated knife
- foam cones (we used three 6" tall cones)
- hot glue gun
- foam balls (we used four 1$^1/_2$" dia. balls)
- air-drying clay (we used Creative Paperclay®)
- tinsel chenille stems
- cream, red, black and orange acrylic paints
- paintbrushes
- flannel scraps
- decoupage glue
- small foam brush
- $^3/_{16}$" dia. black buttons
- $^1/_8$"w ribbon
- clear glitter
- mica flakes (optional)
- paper plate
- plates (ours are 7$^1/_4$" dia.)
- miniature marshmallows, air-dried
- bell jars (ours are 10"h)

These simple snowmen are sure to make you smile!

1. For each snowman, trim away the pointed end of the cone and hot glue a ball on top. Follow manufacturer's instructions to cover the snowman with clay, adding a carrot-shaped nose and smoothing the neck seam with your finger. Poke holes and insert chenille stem arms; allow to dry completely.

2. For the "knit" hat, form a cone shape with clay, press it onto the head and bend it into a hat shape. Allow the hat to dry.

3. For the top hat, cut a cylinder shape from a foam ball and hollow out the bottom. Mold clay around the top and sides of the cylinder. For the brim, press a flat clay circle to the bottom and cut a hole in the center. Slice one sliver at a time from the head until the hat fits well. Allow the hat to dry.

4. Paint the snowmen cream; then, paint the hats and face details. Tie a strip of flannel around a neck for a scarf. Glue buttons to a belly and a ribbon band around the top hat.

5. Brush glue on the snowmen, including the scarves and hats; while wet, sprinkle with glitter (we added mica flakes to the brim of the top hat). Shake the excess onto the paper plate.

6. Place each snowman on a plate surrounded by marshmallows. Cover with a bell jar.

Glittered Snowflake Ornament
(also shown on page 13)
• hot glue gun
• ⁵/₈", ¹/₂" and ¹/₄" dia. wooden beads (we used 6 of each size)
• ³/₄" dia. wooden bead
• sandpaper
• spray primer
• spray paint
• small foam brush
• decoupage glue
• glitter to match paint color
• paper plate
• ¹/₈"w ribbon

Make snowflake ornaments any color you like! Hot glue the ⁵/₈" beads around the large bead, with the holes radiating away from the center. Glue the ¹/₂" beads next, then the small beads, placing one with the hole turned sideways (for the ribbon hanger to go through). Fill in the outer holes with hot glue; sand any rough edges. Prime, then spray paint the ornament in a well-ventilated area; allow to dry. Brush decoupage glue over one side of the snowflake and sprinkle with glitter. Shake the excess onto the paper plate. Repeat to glitter the other side. Tie a ribbon hanger on the ornament.

Kitchen Collection
(also shown on page 17)
Make your kitchen festive with a gathering of white dishes grouped with a backdrop of solid red plates. Place florist's foam in a tureen and arrange greenery in the foam. (If using fresh greenery, moisten the foam before placing it in the tureen.) To add candy cane picks, wrap florist's wire around the bottom of each candy cane and insert the wire in the foam. Fill in with ornaments.

Group assortments of candy canes in a few of the dishes and add greenery and berries as you'd like. Knot ribbon around a peppermint stick, adding mini ornaments and a greenery sprig.

Reverse Appliqué Table Runner
(also shown on page 19)
• ¹/₂ yard of 72"w red felt
• ³/₈ yard of 36"w white felt
• mesh transfer canvas
• water-soluble marking pen
• small sharp scissors
• cotton towel
• fabric glue
• white embroidery floss
• white buttons

1. Cut a 14"x72" red felt piece for the table runner and two 14"x12" white felt pieces for the appliqués.

2. Enlarge the pattern on page 148 to 200%. Use the *Mesh Transfer Canvas Method* (page 144) to transfer the pattern onto each appliqué piece. Carefully cut out the designs. Using the pattern, scallop the ends of the runner. Spritz the pieces with water and blot dry to remove any remaining pen marks.

3. Glue an appliqué piece 1¹/₂" from each end of the runner. Sew buttons to the flower centers and use 6 strands of floss to work *Running Stitches* (page 145) on the runner along the appliqué scallops.

Gingham Apron
(continued from page 21)

7. Baste along the top edge of the skirt. Pull the thread, gathering the skirt to fit the waistband. Pin, then sew the long front edge of the waistband to the skirt front along the gathered edge. Fold and *Whipstitch* the remaining long edge of the waistband to the back.

8. Press the long edges of each tie ¼" to the wrong side twice; topstitch. To form a point at one end of each tie, match long edges and fold the tie in half. Sew across one end. Turn right side out, and matching the seam to the center of the tie, press the sewn end into a point (Fig. 1).

Fig. 1

9. Tuck the raw end of one tie in each end of the waistband, pleating the tie as necessary; topstitch.

10. Matching wrong sides and short edges, fold the pocket fabric in half. Measuring from the fold, mark a 3" tall inverted triangle on the fabric (Fig. 2). Unfold the fabric and fill the white blocks inside the triangle with *Cross Stitches*. Matching right sides and short edges and leaving an opening for turning, fold the fabric in half again and sew the edges together. Turn right side out and press. Use clear nylon thread to sew rickrack along the bottom edges of the triangle. Topstitch the pocket to the apron.

Fig. 2

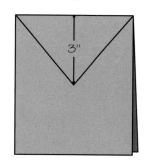

3"

Peppermint Advent Calendar
(continued from page 22)

3. Center and pin one end of a 39" striped ribbon length, wrong side up, 6½" from the top edge of the banner. Sew across the ribbon ½" from the end (Fig. 1), and fold to the right side.

Fig. 1

6½"

4. Arrange a peppermint stick under the ribbon at the sewn end. Tuck and pin the ribbon over the stick to form the first candy holder section. Remove and reposition the stick to pin the next section (Fig. 2). Repeat to pin a total of 25 sections. Sew across the ribbon to secure each section. Trimming any excess, fold the remaining ribbon end ½" to the wrong side and sew to the banner.

Fig. 2

5. For the monogram, use a computer to print a 4" tall letter. Using the letter as a pattern, cut the monogram from red felt and glue to the top of the banner. Work white *Running Stitches* along the edges of the monogram and red *Straight Stitch* stars around it.

6. For the hanging sleeve, cut a 1½"x7½" red felt strip; then, follow Fig. 3 and cut four 1"-long slits. Center the dowel on the back of the banner, 1" from the top. Gluing along the felt edges, adhere the strip to the banner over the dowel.

Fig. 3

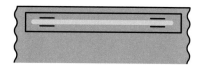

7. For the hanger, thread each end of a 17" white ribbon length through a pair of slits. Fold the ribbon end ½" to the wrong side and topstitch as shown (Fig. 4).

Fig. 4

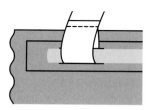

8. Tie a large striped ribbon bow. Adding ornaments, knot white ribbon around the bow. Tack the bow to the bottom of the banner.

9. Slide the peppermint sticks into the candy holder sections. Using narrow ribbons or fibers, tie embellishments to several peppermint sticks.

Ornament Box Treat Holder

(also shown on page 23)

- vintage ornament box with lid and dividers
- craft glue
- 1"w grosgrain ribbon
- scrapbook paper with holiday message
- adhesive foam dots
- Easy Truffles, Candy Bar Fudge and Peppermint Snowball Cookies (page 23)
- red and silver foil wrappers
- snowflake stickers and punch
- white cardstock
- paper candy cups
- clear plastic wrap
- embroidery floss
- tissue paper squares
- vintage-look ornaments

1. Turn the box lid upside down. Glue ribbon around the lid and add a message cut from scrapbook paper to the front with foam dots. Place the box inside the lid.
2. Wrap the truffles and fudge in foil wrappers, adding stickers or punched cardstock snowflakes. Place the truffles in candy cups. Wrap the snowball cookies in plastic wrap and tie a floss bow around each.
3. Line each section of the box with a tissue paper square. Arrange the wrapped treats and the ornaments in the box.

Jolly Frame Set

(continued from page 26)

2. Use your computer to print 5" tall J, O, L, L, Y letters in a cute font. Use removable tape to adhere the letter patterns to cardstock. Cut out the letters with the craft knife. Remove the patterns.
3. Cut and punch scrapbook paper highlights for each letter. Glue the highlights to the letters. Punch several scrapbook paper snowflakes.
4. Use double-sided tape to adhere the letters and snowflakes to the bottom glass pieces. Add the top pieces and replace the glass in the frames.

Girl & Tree Silhouette

(also shown on page 26)

- fine-grit sandpaper
- red spray paint
- unfinished wood frame (5"x7" opening)
- clear acrylic spray sealer
- double-sided removable tape
- red cardstock
- craft knife and cutting mat
- spray adhesive

- scrapbook papers
- ³/₈"w green striped ribbon
- jingle bells
- hot glue gun
- snowflake punch

Use spray paint, sealer and spray adhesive in a well-ventilated area.

1. Lightly sand, then spray paint the frame. Apply sealer to the frame.
2. Enlarge the pattern on page 149 to 142%. Tape the pattern to cardstock. Cut out the image with the craft knife. Remove the pattern.
3. Using spray adhesive, adhere scrapbook paper to the frame backing; trim. Place the backing in the frame and adhere the image to the paper.
4. Wrap ribbon around the frame, add bells and tie a bow. Hot glue the ribbon to the frame back. Using spray adhesive, adhere punched scrapbook paper snowflakes to the frame.

Santa Globes

(also shown on page 28)

- double-sided removable tape
- red cardstock
- craft knife and cutting mat
- scrapbook paper
- 4" dia. clear acrylic separating ball ornaments
- spray adhesive
- clear nylon thread
- ribbon

(continued on page 128)

1. For each globe, photocopy the pattern on page 149 at 100%. Tape the pattern to cardstock. Cut out the image with the craft knife. Remove the pattern.

2. Cut a scrapbook paper circle slightly smaller than the ornament opening. Using spray adhesive in a well-ventilated area, adhere the image to the paper circle. Knot a length of nylon thread through the top of the paper circle, run it through the opening at the top of the ornament and pull tight to bring the paper circle close to the top. Knot it again and trim the excess.

3. Tie ribbon around the ornament, taping as needed to secure.

Felt Ornaments & Tree Topper

(also shown on pages 33 and 34)

- wool felt scraps
- cream cotton yarn
- needle felting tool and mat
- clear nylon thread
- ribbon for hanger
- polyester fiberfill

1. For each ornament, enlarge one of the patterns on page 149 to 225%. For the tree topper, enlarge the pattern to 400%. Using the pattern, cut one felt shape. Follow *Needle Felting* (page 144) to apply the yarn close to the outer edge of the shape; add the "icing" details.

2. Zigzag the felt shape to a piece of felt, adding a ribbon loop at the top and leaving an opening for stuffing. Trim the bottom layer of felt even with the shape.

3. Lightly stuff the shape and sew the opening closed.

Tree Skirt

(also shown on page 34)

- 2⅛ yards each of 72"w cream and brown wool felt (cut into 72"x72" squares)
- 1¾ yards of 72"w tan wool felt (cut into a 60"x60" square)
- string
- water-soluble marking pen
- thumbtack
- clear nylon thread
- red felt
- red and cream cotton yarns
- fabric glue

1. Follow *Making a Fabric Circle* (page 144) and use a 36" string measurement to mark the outer cutting line on the cream felt. Remove the tack and use a 2½" string measurement to mark the inner cutting line.

2. Repeat Step 1, using a 35", then 24" string measurement to mark the cutting lines on the brown felt.

3. Repeat Step 1, using a 29", then 25" string measurement to mark the cutting lines on the tan felt.

4. Cut through all felt layers along the drawn lines. Unfold the circles. Cut a back opening in each circle from the outer edge to the center opening.

5. Aligning the back openings, center and pin the brown circle on the cream skirt 1" from the bottom edge. Center and pin the tan circle on the brown circle 1" from the top edge of the brown. Zigzag the brown and tan circle borders with clear thread.

6. Cut thirteen 4" cream felt circles. Cut thirteen 3½" brown felt circles. Stack and pin the circles to the tan border, placing

them evenly around the skirt. Use cream yarn and work six-point *Straight Stitch* (page 145) snowflakes to attach the stacked circles to the skirt.

7. Pin twelve 1⅛" red felt circles to the tan border between the cream and brown circles. Use red yarn to work *Cross Stitches*, attaching the circles to the tree skirt.

8. Use red yarn to work *Running Stitches* on the brown border, radiating from the cream and brown circles. Use cream yarn to work *Running Stitches* along the edges of the tan border.

9. Wind 39 small balls of red yarn, gluing the yarn end to the ball. Glue or sew the yarn balls to the tree skirt edge.

Gingerbread Cabin

(continued from page 38)

Follow Fig. 1 (page 129) to cut out the dough pieces (make poster board templates if you like). Trim the sides and chimney as shown, cutting away the shaded areas.

Bake at 350 degrees for 9 to 15 minutes or until firm to the touch.

Assembling the Cabin

We used a 12"x12" piece of foam core for the cabin base. Use icing as "glue" on the backs of the gingerbread and candy pieces to adhere them to other pieces, or pipe icing along edges to join pieces, holding the pieces in place or propping them up until the icing begins to harden. Allow icing to harden after each step.

1. Pipe icing for the door, wreath and windows on the cabin front piece and

Fig. 1

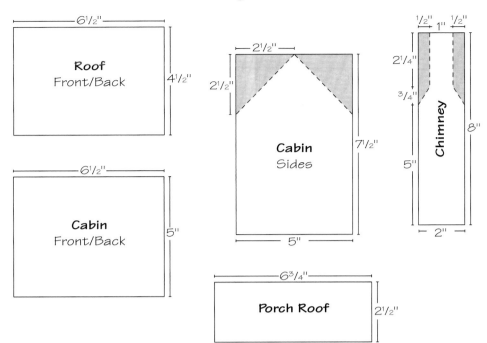

Roof
Front/Back
6½" × 4½"

Cabin
Front/Back
6½" × 5"

Cabin
Sides
2½" 2½" 7½" 5"

Chimney
½" 1" ½" 2¼" ¾" 8" 5" 2"

Porch Roof
6¾" × 2½"

adhere mint candies on the windows and cinnamon candies on the wreath.

2. Piping icing along the short edges, adhere the cabin front, sides and back pieces.

3. Piping icing along the bottom edges, adhere the cabin walls to the center of the base.

4. Adhere 1"x½" chocolate candy pieces to the cabin base for the porch floor.

5. Adhere the front and back roof pieces to the top of the cabin. Adhere the porch roof to the roof front and at the same time adhere the top and bottom of the rolled cookies to support the porch roof.

6. Adhere the chimney to the cabin. Adhere the 1¼"x⅝" chocolate candy pieces to the chimney, breaking the candy pieces as necessary to fit.

7. Use a knife or spatula to spread a thin layer of icing on the roof back; adhere almonds. Repeat for the roof front and porch roof.

8. Pipe icicles and snow on the roof and top of the chimney.

9. Adhere caramel-flavored candies for the "path."

10. Use a knife or spatula to spread icing over the cabin base; sprinkle with sugar sprinkles before the icing hardens.

Fabric Stocking

(also shown on page 45)
- ⅓ yard of stocking fabric
- ¼ yard of solid fabric
- paper-backed fusible web
- ½ yard of pom-pom fringe
- ¼ yard of ⅝"w ribbon for hanger

Match right sides and use a ½" seam allowance unless otherwise indicated.

1. Cut two 5½"x15" cuff pieces from solid fabric. Fuse web to the back of the remaining solid fabric. Enlarge the patterns on page 150 to 328%. Use the patterns and cut 2 stockings, 2 toes and 2 heels from fabrics, cutting one set in reverse.

2. Fuse the heel and toe pieces to the stocking pieces. Machine or hand *Blanket Stitch* (page 145) around the inside edges of the heel and toe pieces.

3. Sew the stocking front and back together, leaving the top edge open.

4. Baste the fringe to one long edge of one cuff piece. Sew the cuff pieces together along this edge; open out flat. Sew the short ends together to form a tube. Press the seam allowances open. Match wrong sides with the fringe at the bottom; press.

5. Matching the cuff seam to the heel-side seam, place the cuff inside the stocking. Matching raw edges, place the hanger between the cuff and stocking at the heel-side seam. Sew the pieces together along the top edge. Turn the cuff to the outside.

Felt Stockings

(also shown on pages 41 and 45)
- ⅓ yard felt for each stocking
- felt scraps for ornaments
- fabric glue
- embroidery floss
- rickrack

1. Enlarge the patterns on page 150 to 335%. For each stocking, use the patterns and cut 2 stockings and 3 ornaments from felt. Cut desired ornament details from felt scraps.

2. Glue the ornament details to the ornaments; let dry.

3. Embellish by working *French Knots, Running Stitches, Stem Stitches* and *Cross Stitches* (page 145) as desired

(continued on page 130)

on each ornament. Work *Stem Stitch* hangers on the stocking front. Glue the ornaments to the stocking front. Add some *Straight Stitch* snowflakes.

4. Sew rickrack along the side and bottom edges of the stocking front.

5. Matching right sides, sew the stocking front and back together along the previously sewn line; turn right side out.

6. Glue rickrack along the top edge of the stocking. Glue a rickrack hanger to the inside of the stocking.

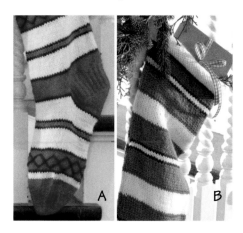

Knit Stockings   ⬛⬛⬜⬜ EASY

(also shown on pages 41 and 45)
Read Knit on pages 146-147 before beginning.

Finished Size: 7" x 27"
    (18 cm x 68.5 cm)

MATERIALS

Medium Weight Yarn
    [3 ounces, 197 yards
    (85 grams, 180 meters)
    per skein]:

Colorway A
Red - 1 skein
Ecru - 1 skein
Green - 1 skein
Dk Green - 1 skein
Brown - 1 skein

Colorway B
Green - 1 skein
Ecru - 1 skein
Red - 1 skein
Dk Green - 1 skein

Straight knitting needles, size 8 (5 mm)
    or size needed for gauge
3 stitch holders
Yarn needle

Gauge: In Stockinette Stitch,
    18 sts and 24 rows =
    4" (10 cm)

Note: Instructions are written for Colorway A with Colorway B in braces { }. Instructions will be easier to read if you circle all the colors pertaining to your colorway. If only one color is given, it applies to both colorways.

LEG
Cuff
With Red {Ecru}, cast on 66 sts.
Row 1: Purl across.
Row 2: Knit across.
Rows 3-20: Repeat Rows 1 and 2, 9 times. Cut yarn.

Body
Row 1: With Ecru {Green}, purl across.
Row 2 (Right side): Knit across.
Row 3: Purl across.
Rows 4-7: Repeat Rows 2 and 3 twice. Cut yarn.
Row 8: With Dk Green, knit across; drop yarn.
Row 9: With Green {Ecru}, purl across.
Row 10: Knit across; cut yarn.
Row 11: With Dk Green, purl across; cut yarn.
Row 12: With Ecru {Green}, knit across.
Row 13: Purl across.
Row 14: Knit across.
Rows 15-20: Repeat Rows 13 and 14, 3 times. Cut yarn.
Row 21: With Brown {Red}, purl across; cut yarn.
Row 22: With Red {Ecru}, knit across.
Row 23: Purl across.
Row 24: Knit across.
Rows 25-30: Repeat Rows 23 and 24, 3 times. Cut yarn.
Row 31: With Brown {Red}, purl across; cut yarn.

Row 32: With Ecru {Green}, knit across.
Row 33: Purl across.
Row 34: Knit across.
Rows 35-40: Repeat Rows 13 and 14, 3 times. Cut yarn.
Row 41: With Dk Green, purl across; drop yarn.
Row 42: With Green {Ecru}, knit across.
Row 43: Purl across; cut yarn.
Row 44: With Dk Green, knit across; cut yarn.
Row 45: With Ecru {Green}, purl across.
Row 46: Knit across.
Row 47: Purl across.
Rows 48-53: Repeat Rows 46 and 47, 3 times. Cut yarn.
Row 54: With Brown {Red}, knit across; cut yarn.
Row 55: With Red {Ecru}, purl across.
Row 56: Knit across.
Row 57: Purl across.
Rows 58-63: Repeat Rows 56 and 57, 3 times. Cut yarn.
Row 64: With Brown {Red}, knit across; cut yarn.
Row 65: With Ecru {Green}, purl across.
Row 66: Knit across.
Row 67: Purl across.
Rows 68-73: Repeat Rows 66 and 67, 3 times.
Rows 74-90: Repeat Rows 8-24.
Rows 91-93: Repeat Rows 23 and 24 once, then repeat Row 23 once **more**. Cut yarn.

HEEL OPTION 1 AS SHOWN ON COLORWAY A
Left Heel
Note: When instructed to slip a stitch, always slip as if to **purl**, unless otherwise instructed.
Row 1: Slip 18 sts onto st holder (Right Heel), slip next 30 sts onto second st holder (Top of Foot), with Red, knit across: 18 sts.
Row 2: Purl across.
Row 3: Slip 1, knit across.
Rows 4-17: Repeat Rows 2 and 3, 7 times.
Heel Turning: P1, P2 tog (Fig. 3, page 146), P1, **turn**; slip 1, K2, **turn**; P2, P2 tog, P1, **turn**; slip 1, K3, **turn**; P3, P2 tog, P1, **turn**; slip 1, K4, **turn**; P4, P2 tog, P1, **turn**; slip 1,

K5, **turn**; P5, P2 tog, P1, **turn**; slip 1, K6, **turn**; P6, P2 tog, P1, **turn**; slip 1, K7, **turn**; P7, P2 tog, P1, **turn**; slip 1, K8, **turn**; P8, P2 tog, P1: 10 sts.

Slip remaining sts onto st holder; cut yarn.

Right Heel

With **right** side facing, slip 18 sts from Right Heel st holder onto empty needle.

Row 1: With Red, knit across.

Row 2: Slip 1, purl across.

Row 3: Knit across.

Rows 4-16: Repeat Rows 2 and 3, 6 times; then repeat Row 2 once **more**.

Heel Turning: K1, K2 tog (Fig. 2, page 146), K1, **turn**; slip 1, P2, **turn**; K2, K2 tog, K1, **turn**; slip 1, P3, **turn**; K3, K2 tog, K1, **turn**; slip 1, P4, **turn**; K4, K2 tog, K1, **turn**; slip 1, P5, **turn**; K5, K2 tog, K1, **turn**; slip 1, P6, **turn**; K6, K2 tog, K1, **turn**; slip 1, P7, **turn**; K7, K2 tog, K1, **turn**; slip 1, P8, **turn**; K8, K2 tog, K1; do **not** cut yarn: 10 sts.

Heel Option 2 as shown on Colorway B

Left Heel

Note: When instructed to slip a stitch, always slip as if to **purl**, unless otherwise instructed.

Row 1: Slip 18 sts onto st holder (Right Heel), slip next 30 sts onto second st holder (Top of Foot), with Ecru, knit across: 18 sts.

Row 2: Purl across.

Row 3: (Slip 1, K1) across.

Rows 4-17: Repeat Rows 2 and 3, 7 times.

Heel Turning: P1, P2 tog (Fig. 3, page 146), P1, **turn**; slip 1, K2, **turn**; P2, P2 tog, P1, **turn**; slip 1, K3, **turn**; P3, P2 tog, P1, **turn**; slip 1, K4, **turn**; P4, P2 tog, P1, **turn**; slip 1, K5, **turn**; P5, P2 tog, P1, **turn**; slip 1, K6, **turn**; P6, P2 tog, P1, **turn**; slip 1, K7, **turn**; P7, P2 tog, P1, **turn**; slip 1, K8, **turn**; P8, P2 tog, P1: 10 sts.

Slip remaining sts onto st holder; cut yarn.

Right Heel

With **right** side facing, slip 18 sts from Right Heel st holder onto empty needle.

Row 1: With Ecru, knit across.

Row 2: (Slip 1, P1) across.

Row 3: Knit across.

Rows 4-16: Repeat Rows 2 and 3, 6 times; then repeat Row 2 once **more**.

Heel Turning: K1, K2 tog (Fig. 2, page 146), K1, **turn**; slip 1, P2, **turn**; K2, K2 tog, K1, **turn**; slip 1, P3, **turn**; K3, K2 tog, K1, **turn**; slip 1, P4, **turn**; K4, K2 tog, K1, **turn**; slip 1, P5, **turn**; K5, K2 tog, K1, **turn**; slip 1, P6, **turn**; K6, K2 tog, K1, **turn**; slip 1, P7, **turn**; K7, K2 tog, K1, **turn**; slip 1, P8, **turn**; K8, K2 tog, K1; do **not** cut yarn: 10 sts.

GUSSET AND INSTEP

Row 1: With **right** side facing, pick up 8 sts along side of Right Heel (Fig. 5, page 147), slip 30 sts from Top of Foot st holder onto an empty needle and knit across, pick up 8 sts along side of Left Heel, knit 10 sts from Left Heel st holder: 66 sts.

Row 2: Purl across.

Row 3: K 16, K2 tog, K 30, slip 1 as if to **knit**, K1, PSSO tog (Fig. 4, page 147), K 16; cut yarn: 64 sts.

Row 4: With Brown {Red}, purl across; cut yarn.

Row 5: With Ecru {Green}, K 15, K2 tog, K 30, slip 1 as if to **knit**, K1, PSSO, K 15: 62 sts.

Row 6: Purl across.

Row 7: K 14, K2 tog, K 30, slip 1 as if to **knit**, K1, PSSO, K 14: 60 sts.

Row 8: Purl across.

Row 9: K 13, K2 tog, K 30, slip 1 as if to **knit**, K1, PSSO, K 13: 58 sts.

Row 10: Purl across.

Row 11: K 12, K2 tog, K 30, slip 1 as if to **knit**, K1, PSSO, K 12: 56 sts.

Row 12: Purl across.

Row 13: K 11, K2 tog, K 30, slip 1 as if to **knit**, K1, PSSO, K 11; cut yarn: 54 sts.

Row 14: With Dk Green, purl across; drop yarn.

Row 15: With Green {Ecru}, K 10, K2 tog, K 30, slip 1 as if to **knit**, K1, PSSO, K 10: 52 sts.

Row 16: Purl across; cut yarn.

Row 17: With Dk Green, knit across; cut yarn.

Row 18: With Ecru {Green}, purl across.

Row 19: Knit across.

Row 20: Purl across.

Rows 21-26: Repeat Rows 19 and 20, 3 times. Cut yarn.

Row 27: With Brown {Red}, knit across; cut yarn.

Row 28: With Red {Ecru}, purl across.

Row 29: Knit across.

Row 30: Purl across.

Rows 31-36: Repeat Rows 29 and 30, 3 times. Cut yarn.

Row 37: With Brown {Red}, knit across; cut yarn.

Row 38: With Ecru {Green}, purl across.

Row 39: Knit across.

Row 40: Purl across; cut yarn.

TOE SHAPING

Row 1: With Red {Ecru}, K 10, K2 tog, K1, place marker, K1, slip 1 as if to **knit**, K1, PSSO, K 20, K2 tog, K1, place marker, K1, slip 1 as if to **knit**, K1, PSSO, K 10: 48 sts.

Row 2: Purl across.

Row 3 (Decrease row): ★ Knit across to within 3 sts of marker, K2 tog, K2, slip 1 as if to **knit**, K1, PSSO; repeat from ★ once **more**, knit across 44 sts.

Row 4: Purl across.

Rows 5-18: Repeat Rows 3 and 4, 7 times: 16 sts.

Bind off all sts in **knit**.

FINISHING

Using photos as a guide, work *Straight Stitch* (page 145) accent lines as desired. With **right** sides together and beginning at Toe, weave seam to 1³/4" (4.5 cm) from top (Fig. 6, page 147); with **wrong** sides together, weave remaining seam. Roll Cuff to **right** side.

Hanging Loop: With Red {Ecru}, cast on 24 sts. Bind off all sts in **knit**. Sew Hanging Loop to inside of Cuff at seam.

Family Photo Wreath
(also shown on page 47)

- floral and craft ring (our wooden ring is 12" dia.)
- fine-grit sandpaper
- acrylic paint
- paintbrush
- unfinished wood discs (ours are $1\frac{1}{2}$", $2\frac{3}{8}$", 3" and $3\frac{3}{4}$" dia.)
- spray adhesive
- black & white photographs (or photocopies)
- scrapbook papers
- circle templates (ours are $1\frac{1}{4}$", $2\frac{1}{8}$", $2\frac{3}{4}$" and $3\frac{1}{2}$" dia.)
- extra-strength craft glue
- mica flakes
- fine-point permanent pen
- jewelry tags
- $\frac{1}{8}$"w and $2\frac{1}{8}$"w ribbons
- medium-gauge wire
- wire cutters
- adhesive foam dots
- jeweled snowflake embellishments

1. Sand, then paint the discs. Using spray adhesive in a well-ventilated area, adhere photos to a few of the discs and scrapbook paper circles to the rest. Glue mica flakes around the edge of some of the circles.
2. For each photo disc, write the year of the photo on a jewelry tag. Knot narrow ribbon through the hole in the tag and glue to the disc.
3. Tie a wire hanger around the ring. Beginning with the largest, arrange the discs on the ring. (If you like, take a digital photo to show placement before removing

the discs for gluing.) Overlapping as desired and using foam dots as needed to support unglued areas, glue the discs in place. Add snowflake embellishments to a few of the discs.
4. Glue a wide-ribbon bow to the front of the wreath.

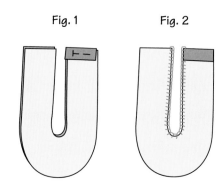

Felt Baby Booties
(continued from page 48)
3. Matching wrong sides, pin each fabric upper to a felt upper, wrapping the long fabric end over the corresponding felt end (Fig. 1). Sew Blanket Stitches (page 145) along the inner curved edge of the layered upper with 3 strands of floss; knot the ends (Fig. 2).

Fig. 1   **Fig. 2**

4. With the felt end on top, overlap the ends $\frac{1}{4}$"; topstitch, adding a second row of stitching close to the first for support (Fig. 3).

Fig. 3

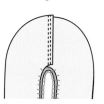

5. Matching wrong sides, pin each lining fabric sole to a felt sole.
6. Match right sides and pin, then sew each upper to a sole using a $\frac{1}{4}$" seam allowance. Trim close to the stitching and turn right side out.
7. Cover the buttons with lining fabric. Securely sew a button and strap to each bootie with floss.

Jazzy Giraffe
(also shown on page 48)

- polka-dot sock (ours is 14" from cuff to toe)
- polyester fiberfill
- pair of striped anklet socks
- four 1" and two $\frac{3}{16}$" dia. buttons
- embroidery floss
- yarn

Small objects can be a choking hazard for babies or small children. Make sure they are securely attached.

1. Turn the dotted sock wrong side out. To form the neck, sew 2 seams along the foot of the sock (Fig. 1).

Fig. 1

2. Trim away the cuff and turn right side out. Stuff the sock and fold the raw edge

under. Work *Running Stitches* (page 145) near the fold; tightly gather the thread and knot the ends.

3. Tack the underside of the head (the sock toe) to the neck (the sock foot).

4. For each leg, cut a 1½"x6" strip from a striped sock. Matching right sides and long edges, use a ¼" seam allowance to sew along the long edge and one short end. Turn the leg right side out and cut off ¾" from the top; set aside the scrap.

5. Stuff the legs. Sew pairs of large buttons and legs to opposite sides of the body, pulling tightly to add shape.

6. Sew 2 leg-scrap "ears" and ³⁄₁₆" button eyes to the head.

7. For the mane, separate the strands and tie floss lengths together in the middle (we used twelve 2" lengths). Sew the mane to the head. For the tail, braid yarn lengths together (we used six 6" lengths). Tie each end with yarn and sew the tail to the body.

Quilted Tote Bag
(also shown on page 49)

- two 7½"x17" pieces of fabric for side pocket sections
- 8"x17" piece of fabric for center pocket section
- 8½"x21" and 21"x27" pieces of lightweight batting
- water-soluble marking pen
- 21"x27" piece each of tote and lining fabric
- two 21" lengths of ³⁄₈"w rickrack
- 2¾ yards of 1¼"w twill tape
- clear nylon thread
- four 1⅛" dia. self-covered buttons

Use a ½" seam allowance unless otherwise indicated.

1. For the pocket, match long edges and sew the side pocket pieces to the center pocket piece; press seam allowances open. Matching wrong sides and long edges, press the pocket in half; unfold wrong side up. Pin the 8½"w batting piece to the lower half of the fabric; baste (Fig. 1).

Fig. 1

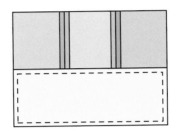

2. Matching right sides, sew the long pocket edges together; turn right side out and press. Use a ruler and marking pen to mark an X from corner to corner of each fabric section; sew along drawn lines through all layers to quilt.

3. Baste the 21"w batting piece to the wrong side of the tote fabric. Follow Fig. 2 to pin the pocket (with the seam at the bottom) to the right side of the tote fabric. Topstitch along the bottom edge of the pocket through all layers as shown in blue. Baste rickrack ¾" from each end of the tote piece.

Fig. 2

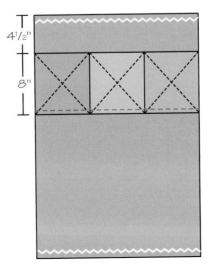

4. Beginning where shown (Fig. 3), pin twill tape to the tote piece, allowing for a 21" handle loop at each end of the tote. Overlapping the tape ends, fold the top end under ½" (trim if needed) and pin in place. Topstitch the tape to the tote piece along each long edge of the tape, stopping and starting 1" from the short ends of the tote fabric.

Fig. 3

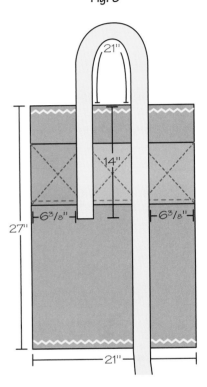

5. Matching right sides and short ends, fold the tote piece in half; sew the sides together. To form the bottom corners, sew across each corner 1" from the point (Fig. 4). Turn the tote right side out.

Fig. 4

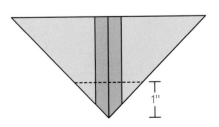

(continued on page 134)

133

6. Leaving an opening in one side seam for turning, repeat to sew the lining sides together and to form the bottom corners; do not turn right side out. Place the tote inside the lining and pin the top edges together. Sew along the top edges, being careful not to catch the handles in the stitching. Turn right side out and sew the opening closed. Tuck the lining inside the tote and press. Use clear nylon thread to zigzag along the top edge of the tote, catching the rickrack and handles in the stitching.

7. Cover the buttons with pocket fabric scraps and sew a button near one top back corner of the tote. Finger pleat the side of the tote and run the needle through all layers to the tote front. Sew a second button to the top front corner and run the needle back through all layers. Pull the thread tight and tie at the back to secure the pleat. Repeat at the opposite corner with the remaining buttons.

Knit Pillow

 **EASY**

(also shown on page 50)
Read Knit on pages 146-147
before beginning.

Finished Size: 14" (35.5 cm) square

MATERIALS

Medium Weight Yarn

[3 ounces, 185 yards
(85 grams, 170 meters)
per skein]:

Lt Green - 3 skeins

Green - 1 skein

Straight knitting needles, size 7
(4.5 mm) **or** size needed for gauge
3 bobbins
14" (35.5 cm) square pillow form
Yarn needle
Felt scrap
Pinking shears
Sewing needle and thread
Holiday napkin (ours is 8"x8¹/₂"/
20.5 cm x 21.5 cm)
4 assorted vintage buttons
Purchased crocheted doily (ours is
6¹/₄"/16 cm dia.)

Gauge: In Stockinette Stitch,
20 sts and 28 rows =
4" (10 cm)

FRONT

Bottom Border

With Lt Green, cast on 78 sts.
Row 1: (K1, P1) across.
Row 2: (P1, K1) across.
Rows 3-22: Repeat Rows 1 and 2,
10 times.

Center

Wind a small amount of Green onto one bobbin and a small amount of Lt Green onto 2 bobbins. Wind more yarn onto bobbins as needed.
Row 1 (Right side): (K1, P1) 8 times, with Green K 46 (see *Changing Colors*, page 146), with Lt Green (K1, P1) across.
Row 2: (P1, K1) 8 times, with Green P 46, with Lt Green (P1, K1) across.
Rows 3 and 4: Repeat Rows 1 and 2.
Row 5: (K1, P1) 8 times, with Green K3, with Lt Green K 40, with Green K3, with Lt Green (K1, P1) across.
Row 6: (P1, K1) 8 times, with Green P3, with Lt Green P 40, with Green P3, with Lt Green (P1, K1) across.
Rows 7-60: Repeat Rows 5 and 6, 27 times.
Cut center Lt Green and left side Green.
Rows 61-64: Repeat Rows 1 and 2 twice.
Cut Green and left side Lt Green.
Row 65: (K1, P1) 8 times, K 46, (K1, P1) across.

Top Border

Row 1: (P1, K1) across.
Row 2: (K1, P1) across.
Rows 3-21: Repeat Rows 1 and 2, 9 times; then repeat Row 1 once **more**.
Bind off all sts in pattern.

BACK

Work same as Front.

Sew 3 sides of the Front and Back together. Insert the pillow form and sew the remaining side closed.

Cut four 1¹/₂" (4 cm) diameter felt circles with pinking shears. Sew the holiday napkin, felt circles and buttons to the Front. Sew the doily to the Back.

Fringed Throw

(also shown on page 51)
• fleece throw
• 1"w grosgrain ribbon
• yarns (we chose 7 colors)
• ¹/₈"w silk ribbon (we chose
2 colors)

1. For the fringe base, cut grosgrain ribbon the width of the throw plus 1".
2. Cut a 2-yard length of each yarn and silk ribbon. Hold the lengths together and fold them in half.
3. Beginning ¹/₂" from one end of the base ribbon, zigzag the yarn/ribbon bundle to the base ribbon, so the loose (fringe) ends of the bundle extend about 6" beyond the long edge of the base (Fig. 1).

Fig. 1

fringe

4. Leaving the needle in the ribbon, trim the bundle along the top long edge of the base.

5. Align the new bundle ends beside the sewn fringe ends and zigzag this next section to the base. Trim along the top long edge.

6. Continue sewing fringe to the base, cutting new 2-yard long bundles as needed, and stopping $1/2$" from the remaining base end.

7. Folding the base ribbon ends to the wrong side, pin, then zigzag the ribbon side of the fringe to one end of the throw. Trim the fringe.

Felt Birds
(continued from page 54)
Use a $1/4$" seam allowance.

1. For each bird, use the patterns on page 152 and cut 2 birds and one of each remaining pattern piece from felt.

2. Follow *Transferring Patterns* (page 144) to transfer the design to each wing. Use 2 strands of floss and work *Stem Stitch* (page 145) flowers and stems. Sew beads to the flower centers.

3. Accordion-fold the straight edge of the tail and baste to secure. Sew beads along the scalloped edge. With the folds at the top, sew the basted edge of the tail to the end of one bird piece; fold and sew the beak to the head (Fig. 1).

Fig. 1

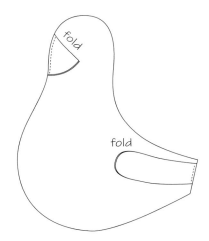

fold

fold

4. Loop a 6" ribbon and knot the ends together. Matching raw edges, sew the loop to the top back of the bird.

5. Matching right sides, sew the bird pieces together, leaving an opening for turning. Turn right side out, stuff and sew the opening closed. Sew the wings and button eyes to the bird.

Charm & Button Bracelet
(also shown on page 54)
• 5mm jump rings
• needle- and round-nose pliers
• vintage shank buttons
• assorted charms
• link bracelet
• assorted beads
• 2" headpins
• wire cutters
• craft glue
• scrapbook papers
• flip-top box with window lid
  (ours is $6^3/8$"x$6^3/8$"x$1^1/2$")
• large-eye needle
• 22-gauge white plastic-coated wire
• tag punch (optional)
• $1/4$"w silk ribbon
• $1/8$" dia. hole punch
• hot glue gun
• adhesive foam dot

Read Working with Jump Rings on page 146 before beginning.

Use jump rings to attach buttons and charms to the bracelet. Thread one or more beads on each headpin; trim the pin $1/4$" from the last bead and tightly loop the pin end onto the bracelet with round-nose pliers.

Layer and glue scrapbook papers together to fit in the box. Using the needle to pierce holes in the paper, secure the bracelet to the center of the paper with wire. Place the paper in the box.

Punch or cut a tag from scrapbook paper. Thread silk ribbon through a hole punched at one end. Hot glue buttons and a charm to the tag; then, secure it to the box lid with a foam dot.

Glittered Houses

(also shown on page 55)

- one-piece fold-out brown gift boxes (we used three 2"hx3"wx3"d and one 4"hx4"wx4"d)
- craft glue
- ruler, craft knife and cutting mat
- cream and assorted colors of cardstock
- thin cardboard sheets
- scallop-edged scissors
- tracing paper
- miniature wreath
- rickrack
- disposable foam brush
- decoupage glue
- fine glitter
- mica flakes
- spray adhesive
- white felt
- cake stand (ours is 10½" dia.)
- miniature bottle brush trees
- vintage miniature ornaments

1. Leaving the bottom of each gift box open, fold and glue the lid flap closed. Turn the box top-side down.
2. For the roof decking, fold the straight-sided flaps together so they touch in the center. Mark the roof angles on each roof tab (Fig. 1); then, lightly score the lines with the ruler and craft knife. Cut out a V-shaped notch from the top of each roof tab to the point of the roof decking (Fig. 2).

Fig. 1

Fig. 2

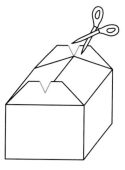

3. Unfold the roof decking. Fold the roof tabs to the inside along the scored lines and glue the decking flaps to the tabs.
4. For the large house, glue cream cardstock to cardboard and cut a roof 1" larger then the roof decking on all sides. Score and fold the roof in the center and glue it to the house. Repeat for the small houses, cutting each roof about ½" larger than the decking on all sides, and using scallop-edged scissors where desired.
5. Accordion-fold a 1½"x2½" cardboard piece and glue the "steps" to the large house.
6. Use the patterns on page 152 and follow the photos to cut out and glue cardstock doors and windows to the houses (we glued the miniature wreath to a solid door). Cut out cardboard chimneys and cardstock-covered chimney caps. Fold each chimney along the dashed lines with the tabs to the inside; glue on the cap. Glue chimneys to roofs as desired. Glue a 1"x3" cardstock-covered porch roof to the large house.

7. Cover the work surface. Glue rickrack along roof edges where you'd like. Brush decoupage glue on the sides and roof of each house; sprinkle with fine glitter, tap off the excess and allow to dry. Brush more glue on each roof and chimney cap; sprinkle with mica flakes and tap off the excess.
8. Apply spray adhesive in a well-ventilated area to wavy-edged felt circles (ours are about 15" diameter) and sprinkle with mica flakes. Placing one circle on the cake stand, arrange the houses, trees and vintage ornaments on the circles.

Oven Mitt Set

(also shown on page 56)

- thick terry bath towel
- ⅜ yard of fabric for backing and bias binding
- vintage holiday tea towel
- water-soluble marking pen
- 18" ruler
- tissue paper
- two ⅝" dia. buttons
- favorite cookie recipe printed on cardstock
- paper-backed fusible web
- coordinating fabric scraps
- pinking shears
- wire whisk and cookie cutters

1. For each mitt, cut an 8½" square each from the terry towel and backing fabric. Cut one 6"x8½" piece each from the terry and tea towels. Cut a 2"w bias strip 52" long (this strip will need to be pieced).

2. For each mitt backing, use the marking pen and ruler to mark a diagonal grid on the right side of the backing fabric square (our lines are about 1½" apart) (Fig. 1). Repeat on the vintage towel piece for the pocket front.

Fig. 1

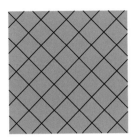

3. Matching wrong sides, stack and pin the mitt backing on the terry square. Place tissue paper under the terry square (to keep the terry from catching) and sew along the marked lines through both thicknesses to quilt. Carefully remove the tissue paper. Repeat to sew the pocket front to the remaining terry piece.

4. With terry sides together and matching bottom edges, pin the pocket to the mitt. Cutting through all layers, round the corners; unpin. Zigzag around the mitt edges, then the pocket edges. Spritz with water to remove the pen lines.

5. Press each long edge of the bias strip ½" to the center and fold in half lengthwise; cut off an 8½"-long piece. Sandwiching the pocket top edge in the fold, sew the short bias binding to the pocket. Baste the pocket to the mitt.

6. Beginning at the top right corner and sandwiching the mitt edges in the fold, sew the long bias binding around the mitt, overlapping the ends; do not trim. Continue to sew the long edges of the binding together to form the hanger. Fold the short end ¼" to the wrong side and sew the hanger end and button to the mitt.

7. For the recipe card, fuse the fabric scraps together and pink the edges ¼" larger than the recipe card on all sides. Zigzag the card to the pinked fabric and tuck the recipe, whisk and cookie cutters in the mitts.

Crochet Kitty Toy
(continued from page 58)

Rnd 4: (2 Sc in next sc, sc in next 2 sc) around: 24 sc.

Rnd 5: (Sc in next 3 sc, 2 sc in next sc) around: 30 sc.

Rnd 6: (2 Sc in next sc, sc in next 4 sc) around: 36 sc.

Rnd 7: (Sc in next 5 sc, 2 sc in next sc) around: 42 sc.

Rnd 8: Sc in each sc around.

Rnd 9: Sc in each sc around; slip st in next st, finish off; do **not** remove marker.

Rnd 10: With **right** side facing, join Ecru with sc in same st as joining (see *Joining with Sc, page 147*); sc in each sc around; slip st in next st, finish off; do **not** remove marker.

Rnd 11: With **right** side facing, join Purple with sc in same st as joining; sc in each sc around.

Rnd 12: Sc in each sc around.

Rnd 13: Sc in each sc around; slip st in next st, finish off; do **not** remove marker.

Rnd 14: With **right** side facing, join Ecru with sc in same st as joining; sc in each sc around; slip st in next st, finish off; do **not** remove marker.

Rnd 15: With **right** side facing, join Green with sc in same st as joining; sc in each sc around.

Rnd 16: Sc in each sc around.

Rnd 17: Sc in each sc around; slip st in next st, finish off; do **not** remove marker.

Rnd 18: With **right** side facing, join Ecru with sc in same st as joining; sc in each sc around; slip st in next st, finish off; do **not** remove marker.

Rnd 19: With **right** side facing, join Yellow with sc in same st as joining; sc in each sc around.

Rnd 20: Sc in each sc around.

To work sc decrease (uses next 2 sc), pull up a loop in next 2 sc, YO and draw through all 3 loops on hook.

Rnd 21: (Sc in next 5 sc, sc decrease) around: 36 sc.

Rnd 22: (Sc decrease, sc in next 4 sc) around: 30 sc.

Rnd 23: (Sc in next 3 sc, sc decrease) around: 24 sc.

Rnd 24: (Sc decrease, sc in next 2 sc) around: 18 sc.

Stuff Ball with polyester fiberfill.

Rnd 25: (Sc in next sc, sc decrease) around: 12 sc.

Rnd 26: Sc decrease around; slip st in next sc, finish off leaving a long end for sewing: 6 sc.

Thread needle with long end, weave needle through sts on Rnd 26, gather **tightly** and secure end.

FINISHING
Leaving a 4" tail at the bottom, run the two 10" ribbons through the ball. Run the top ends back into the ball to secure and knot each bottom end.

Leaving a 4" tail at the bottom, run the 1⅝-yard ribbon through the ball. Tie a knot at the bottom end and knot the ribbons together just below the ball. Thread the bell on the ribbon above the ball. Glue the loose ribbon end to one end of the dowel. Wrap the ribbon around the dowel to the opposite end and knot the ribbon to itself, securing it to the dowel.

Wrapping Station

(also shown on page 61)

Gather holiday wrap, ribbons, trims & tags and organize a wrapping station (we attached a vintage mailbox and a wire screen to the wall above the table for extra storage). Keep your supplies in holiday tins and galvanized containers with festive labels. With your own wrapping station, you'll always be ready to wrap!

Wrap-in-a-Snap

(also shown on page 62)

Gather tissue or wrapping paper around an odd-shaped gift with a pretty ribbon bow. Tie a cardstock tag with a rub-on message to a basket or tote and place the package inside. Two-gifts-in-one!

Rickrack Wrap

(also shown on pages 62 and 63)

Add pizzazz to your gift-wrapped box. Adhere rickrack lengths around the box with glue or double-sided tape. Use wavy-edged scissors to cut cardstock to cover the top of the package. Cut a center

slit near each edge a little wider than your ribbon. Thread the ends of one ribbon through slits on opposite ends of the cardstock topper and adhere the ribbon ends under the package. Run another ribbon under the box and thread the ends up through the remaining slits, catch the first ribbon and tie a bow at the top.

Punched Snowflake Sack

(also shown on page 66)

- brown gift bag (ours is 8"x10½")
- 1" snowflake punch
- assorted hole punches
- scrapbook paper
- craft glue
- jute twine
- vintage buttons
- lacy trim
- emery board or fine-grit sandpaper
- rub-on holiday message and alphabet
- 2 jewelry tags
- thread

1. Leaving the bag closed, pinch the front and one front side together and punch 4 snowflakes through both layers. Repeat on the other side. Set the flakes aside. Punch tiny holes above and below the flake-shaped holes on the bag.

2. Punch 8 scrapbook paper snowflakes. Gently fold the long branches of the flakes toward the center. Working from the inside of the bag out, insert each folded flake through the center of a flake-shaped hole on the bag front and rotate the flake slightly, so the long branches cover the short branch holes in the bag. Unfold the

long branches for a dimensional effect and glue or use twine to sew a button to the center of each flake.

3. Sew trim around the top of the bag using twine and Running Stitches (page 145). Punch holes in the bag to accent the trim.

4. For the tag, cut a scrapbook paper strip (ours is 1¾"x8") and sand the edges. Punch a snowflake from the bottom, and follow Step 2 to insert and rotate one of the bag snowflakes. Glue trim along the tag edges; fold the tag in half. Add a rub-on message to the front. Add buttons. Personalize the jewelry tags with rub-ons and use thread to hang them from the lower button.

Chipboard Snowflake Sack

(also shown on page 66)

- assorted hole punches
- brown gift bag (ours is 5¼"x8⅝")
- ribbon scrap
- craft glue
- button
- 1" snowflake punch
- scrapbook papers
- alphabet stamps
- ink pad
- 2 jewelry tags
- thread
- 3" chipboard snowflakes
- brown paper lunch bag
- 1/16" dia. anywhere hole punch (optional)

1. Punch holes through the top front of the bag. Tie a ribbon through 2 holes.

2. Glue a button and a punched scrapbook paper snowflake to the bag. Stamp the tags and use thread to hang them from the button.

3. Glue scrapbook paper to the chipboard snowflakes; trim. Glue snowflakes punched from the lunch bag and scrapbook paper to the covered chipboard flakes. Add punched circles and snowflake branches where desired. (We used an anywhere punch to make holes in the center snowflake.) Glue the snowflakes to the gift bag, trimming the flakes to fit.

Fig. 3

5. Continue to make 18 more loops. Secure the bow with wire. Trim the streamers and fluff up the loops. Add the bow to ribbon tied around the wrapped gift.

Surprise Jewelry Box
(also shown on page 68)
- transfer paper
- double-sided cardstock
- stylist or bone folder
- double-sided tape
- fabric glue
- rickrack
- twill tape
- piece of jewelry (for gift)
- 2 decorative brads
- assorted ribbons
- photocopy of a 1" dia. black & white photo
- glittered wreath frame sticker (found with scrapbooking supplies)

1. Enlarge the pattern on page 154 to 200%. Transfer the pattern to cardstock and cut out. Score, then fold the box along the dashed lines. Tape the long flap to the wrong side of the opposite long edge, forming a triangular tube.
2. For the jewelry card, cut a 1⅝"x5⅝" cardstock strip. Center and glue an 11" rickrack length on a 10" length of twill tape. Threading the jewelry piece to the center, fold the twill tape in half. Attach the folded tape to the cardstock strip with a brad.
3. Insert the jewelry card in the box and tuck in the ends. Embellish the box with twill tape, ribbons and rickrack. Adhere the photocopy to the frame sticker and use a brad to attach it to the twill tape.

Floral Bow
(continued from page 69)
2. Gather the ribbon between your thumb and forefinger at the streamer mark. Twist the remaining ribbon one full turn (Fig. 1).

Fig. 1

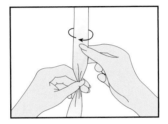

3. To make the first loop, place the first loop mark behind the streamer mark; gather the ribbon and twist the remaining ribbon one full turn (Fig. 2).

Fig. 2

4. Place the second loop mark behind the first loop mark; gather and twist the remaining ribbon one full turn (Fig. 3).

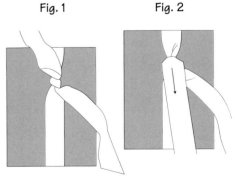

Necktie Bow with Photo Tag
(continued from page 69)
1. Follow Fig. 1 to knot the ribbon around the wrapped gift, leaving a short streamer (about 9") at the top and a long streamer (about 10") at the bottom. Fold the short streamer down (Fig. 2).

Fig. 1   Fig. 2

(continued on page 140)

2. Fold the long streamer over the top and behind the knot (Figs. 3 and 4). Tuck the long streamer through the loop and pull, forming the necktie bow (Figs. 5 and 6). Trim the ends.

Fig. 3

Fig. 4

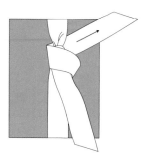

Fig. 5

Fig. 6

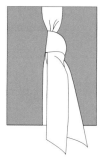

3. For the tag, stamp a deckle-edged white cardstock tag with background words using distressing ink. Use photo corners to attach the photo to a red cardstock "ribbon." Place the "ribbon" on the tag and cut a tiny slit through both cardstock layers for the button shank. Insert the shank through the slit and secure on the back with the paperclip. Clip the tag to the ribbon on the package.

Lollipop Bottle

(also shown on page 73)
• tracing paper
• cream cardstock
• striped scrapbook paper
• craft glue
• rub-on holiday message
• glitter
• 1/2"w silk ribbon
• double-sided tape
• vintage milk bottle
• Candy Tree Lollipops (page 73)
• small plastic bags
• green floral tape
• wooden skewers
• 1/8" dia. hole punch
• candy-coated chocolates

This gift is sure to delight! Use the label patterns on page 154 and cut cardstock and scrapbook paper label pieces. Layer and glue the pieces together. Add the rub-on message and glitter. Thread ribbon through slits cut in the label. Add a little tape on the back and tie the label around the bottle.

For the tags, glue a scrapbook paper piece to a cardstock piece. Use the tag pattern and cut a tag for each lollipop.

Place a plastic bag over each lollipop. To lengthen the "trunks," wrap green floral tape around a wooden skewer and each lollipop stick, catching the bag ends to seal. Thread ribbon through a hole punched in the tag and tie it around the stick. Fill the bottle with candy-coated chocolates and insert the lollipops.

Breakfast Ring Wrap

(also shown on page 76)
• tracing paper
• green and cream cardstock
• craft knife and cutting mat
• 1/8" and 1/4" dia. hole punches
• spray adhesive
• ribbons and mini rickrack
• Cranberry Breakfast Rings (page 76)
• Gooseberry Patch's Merry Christmas Enamelware Plates
• cellophane
• twist ties

For each breakfast ring, use the pattern on page 153 and cut a green tag and use the craft knife and punches to cut a cream wreath design. In a well-ventilated area, adhere the wreath to the tag with spray adhesive. Tie ribbons and rickrack through a hole punched in the tag. To gift wrap, place the breakfast ring on a plate, wrap with cellophane and close with a twist tie. Tie the tag around the twist tie.

Soup Dinner Kit

(also shown on page 77)

- rustic wood box (ours is 14¹/₂"lx7¹/₂"wx4"h)
- ivory acrylic paint
- paintbrush
- ³/₄"w pre-printed twill tape (ours says "special delivery")
- double-sided tape
- wrapping paper
- 28-oz. can crushed tomatoes
- cream cardstock
- oval templates (ours are 2¹/₂" and 3" long)
- red pencil
- jars of Italian Soup Mix (page 77)
- scallop-edged scissors
- black fine-point permanent pen
- mini alphabet stencil
- removable tape
- fresh bread
- 2 dishtowels
- bowls
- soup spoons

1. Drybrush the box with ivory paint to give it a worn look; allow to dry. Tie a twill tape bow around the box.

2. Tape wrapping paper around the side of the tomato can. Cut a round cardstock label for the can top. Use the templates and red pencil to make oval labels for the can, soup mix jars and box; cut out, scalloping the edges.

3. Use the pen and stencil to write names on the labels. Write the instructions to make the soup on the underside of the round label and adhere it to the top of the can with removable tape. Use double-sided tape to attach the remaining labels.

4. Tie a twill tape bow around bread wrapped up in a dishtowel. Tuck the remaining towel, bowls, spoons and soup mix in the box.

Muffin Picks and Box

(also shown on page 78)

- ¹/₈" and 1" dia. circle punches
- red and white cardstock
- craft glue
- red and white embroidery floss
- sharp needle
- toothpicks
- Raspberry-Filled Muffins (page 78)
- assorted ribbons for ties
- wrapping paper
- one-piece fold-out pastry box (ours is 9"x9"x4")
- spray adhesive
- craft knife and cutting mat
- tracing paper
- two 1"w grosgrain ribbons
- rub-on letters
- ¹/₈"w ribbon
- small safety pin

Use 3 strands of floss for all stitching.

1. For each muffin pick, punch two 1" cardstock circles. Gluing the floss ends to the back, work a *Straight Stitch* (page 145) snowflake on one circle. Sandwiching a toothpick in between, glue the circles together. Insert the pick in a muffin and tie a ribbon around the muffin cup.

2. In a well-ventilated area, adhere wrapping paper to the flat box with spray adhesive. Trim the excess paper and fold into a box shape. Add the muffins.

3. Use the patterns on page 155 and cut a cardstock tag and "buckle." Punch a ¹/₈" hole in the tag. Cut slits and use the needle to pierce holes in the buckle where shown. Work *Running Stitches* around the buckle. Cutting each 1"w ribbon to fit, wrap the ribbons around the box. Weave the ribbons though the buckle and glue the ends to the back of the buckle.

4. Add rub-ons and work a *Straight Stitch* snowflake on the tag. Tie a ¹/₈"w ribbon bow to the pin and pin the tag to the 1"w ribbon.

Fondue Kit

(also shown on page 78)

- tissue paper
- water-soluble marking pen (optional)
- 9¹/₂"x10¹/₂" cream muslin piece
- brown, blue, red and orange embroidery floss
- ¹/₄ yard of red ticking fabric
- fabric glue
- grosgrain ribbon (we used ³/₈"w and ⁵/₈"w)
- canvas bin (ours measures 13"lx10"wx7¹/₂"h at the top)
- 8 buttons

(continued on page 142)

- cellophane bags of dipping items
- fondue pot and forks
- jar of Mom's Chocolate Fondue (page 78)
- wood excelsior

Use 3 strands of floss for all stitching.

1. Follow *Transferring Patterns* (page 144) to transfer the design on page 154 onto muslin. Work *Stem Stitch* (page 145) outlines and letters, *Straight Stitch* snowflakes and *French Knot* eyes and buttons. Trim the stitched piece to 5¼"x6¼". Center and zigzag the stitched piece on a 6¼"x7¼" piece of ticking.
2. Glue ribbon around the bin and on the handles. Use floss to sew buttons to the handle ends and to catch the corners of the stitched piece on front of the bin.
3. Tie strips of ticking around the bags and fondue forks. Use ribbon to tie a square of ticking around the jar lid. Line the bin with excelsior and add the fondue pot with all the trimmings.

Cupfuls of Truffles

(also shown on page 79)
- assorted teacups (we found ours at the flea market)
- cellophane bags
- Cookies & Cream Truffles, Mocha Truffles and Peanut Butter-Cocoa Truffles (page 79)
- ½"w ribbon
- cardstock
- scallop-edged scissors
- rub-on letters

- clear adhesive dots
- tracing paper
- clear dome alphabet stickers
- raffia
- jute twine
- ⅛" dia. hole punch
- craft glue
- scrapbook paper
- miniature clothespins

For each cup, fill a cellophane bag with a truffle assortment and tie with ribbon. Cut a 5" diameter cardstock circle and scallop the edge. Add a rub-on message to the outer edge of the circle. Adhere the circle to the bottom of the cup with an adhesive dot.

Using the pattern on page 155, cut a tag from cardstock. Use a sticker to add a monogram and tie raffia and twine through the punched hole. Glue scrapbook paper to one side of the clothespin and clip the tag to the ribbon.

Brownie Plate

(also shown on page 80)
- vintage plate
- jadite eggcup
- clear adhesive dots
- scallop-edged scissors
- patterned food tissue paper
- acrylic paint
- paintbrush
- 3" dia. wooden disc
- craft glue
- scrapbook paper
- cardstock
- rub-on holiday message
- clear dimensional adhesive glaze

- mica flakes
- ⅝"w ribbon
- Creamy Peppermint Brownies (page 80)
- cellophane bag

Create a one-of-a-kind cake plate using a vintage plate and eggcup. Simply adhere the plate to the rim of the eggcup with adhesive dots. Then line the plate with a scallop-edged tissue circle.

For the tag, paint the disc; then, layer and glue scrapbook paper and cardstock circles to the front. Add the rub-on message. Apply glaze to the tag and allow to dry. Run a bead of glue along the edge of the tag and sprinkle with mica flakes. Glue the tag to a ribbon bow with long streamers.

Place the brownies in the bag and tie closed with ribbon. Adhere the tag and place the brownies on the plate.

Caramel Corn Cone

(also shown on page 80)
- vintage napkin or hankie (ours is 12"x13")
- double-sided removable tape
- cardstock
- plastic wrap
- liquid starch
- straight pin
- ¼"w ribbon
- cone-shaped icing bag
- No-Fuss Caramel Corn (page 80)
- vintage ornaments and tag
- embroidery floss

1. Fold the napkin once diagonally; then, pull the top center point a few inches to the right so the points don't align (Fig. 1).

Fig. 1

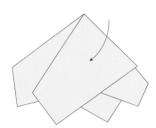

2. Fold the napkin from right to left, making sure the points don't align (Fig. 2).

Fig. 2

3. Roll and tape cardstock into a cone shape; trim the wide end so it will stand when placed upside down. (Our cone is 7¹/₂" tall with a 3" diameter…for a different size napkin, adjust the length of the cone so it's a few inches shorter than your folded-up napkin.) Adjust the diameter of the cone if needed so the folded napkin will wrap around it with about 1" overlap. Set the napkin aside and cover the cone with plastic wrap. Place a piece of plastic wrap on the table.

4. Dip the folded napkin into a bowl of starch. Squeeze out the excess starch. Overlap and wrap the napkin around the cone. Pin the napkin "seam" together at the top point. Stand the napkin and cone on the plastic wrap with the corners of the napkin draping onto the table; allow to dry overnight. Remove the pin and cone from the stiffened napkin. Sew a ribbon hanger to the cone.

5. Fill the icing bag with caramel corn and tie closed with ribbon. Add ornaments and a tag with floss. Place the bag in the cone.

Turtle Box

(also shown on page 81)

For each box of goodies, cover a box bottom (ours is 4"x4"x2¹/₂") with holiday wrapping paper.

Fill a cellophane bag with Caramel Turtles (page 81) and close with a twist tie. Place the candy in the box. Tie ribbon around the package, adding a bow at the top. Attach an oval cardstock tag stamped with a holiday greeting and your quick & tasty gift is ready to go.

Take-Out Boxes

(also shown on page 81)

For each treat box, line a colorful take-out container with patterned tissue paper. Fill a cellophane bag with Party Mix (page 81) and close with a twist tie. Knot ribbon around the bag and place it in the container.

Cover a purchased tag with scrapbook paper. Tuck a handwritten cardstock label in a purchased mini mitten (a knit, crochet or felt mitten will look great). Use double-sided tape to attach the mitten to the tag and tie it to the container with jute twine…oh-so cute!

Cookie Holders

(also shown on page 83)

• double-sided cardstock
• scallop-edged scissors (optional)
• double-sided tape
• rub-on letters
• 1¹/₂" dia. circle punch
• ¹/₈" dia. hole punch
• assorted ribbons
• bottled coffee drinks
• White Chocolate-Cranberry Cookies (page 82)
• plastic wrap

Enlarge the patterns on page 155 to 196%. For each holder, use the patterns and cut a cardstock cookie holder and scallop-edged valance (we cut our valance following the scallop design printed on our cardstock). Discard the cookie window and bottle opening pieces. Fold on the dashed lines. Tape the flap to the holder along the top fold line. Tape the valance to the holder above the window.

Add a rub-on name to a punched tag and tie it to the holder with ribbons. Tape a punched circle to the bottle lid and slip the cookie holder over the neck. Wrap a cookie in plastic wrap and insert it in the holder.

General Instructions

Making Patterns

Place tracing or tissue paper over the pattern and draw over the lines. For a more durable pattern, use a permanent marker to draw over the pattern on stencil plastic.

Sizing Patterns

To change the size of the pattern, divide the desired height or width of the pattern (whichever is greater) by the actual height or width of the pattern. Multiply the result by 100 and photocopy the pattern at this percentage.

For example: You want your pattern to be 8"h, but the pattern on the page is 6"h. So 8÷6=1.33x100=133%. Copy the pattern at 133%.

Transferring Patterns

Pick the transfer method that works best with the fabric and project you've chosen. If you choose a method using a water-soluble pen, check first on a scrap piece to make sure the floss or felt colors won't bleed when you remove the pen markings.

Tissue Paper Method

Trace the pattern onto tissue paper. Pin the tissue paper to the felt or fabric and stitch through the paper. Carefully tear the tissue paper away.

Water-Soluble Marking Pen Method

Trace the pattern onto tissue paper. Tape the tissue pattern and fabric to a sunny window; then, trace the pattern onto the fabric with the pen. Embroider the design.

Lightly spritz the finished design with water to remove any visible pen markings.

Mesh Transfer Canvas Method

Trace the pattern onto tissue paper and place mesh transfer canvas over the pattern. Using a permanent marker, trace the pattern onto the canvas. Place the marked canvas on the felt or fabric and draw over the pattern with a water-soluble marking pen, leaving a dashed line on the felt or fabric. After needle felting, stitching or cutting out the design, dampen any areas where the marking pen shows with a cotton or paper towel or a cotton swab to remove the marks.

Making a Fabric Circle

Matching right sides, fold the fabric square in half from top to bottom and again from left to right. Tie one end of a length of string to a water-soluble marking pen; insert a thumbtack through the string at the length indicated in the project instructions. Insert the thumbtack through the folded corner of the fabric. Holding the tack in place and keeping the string taut, mark the cutting line (Fig. 1).

Fig. 1

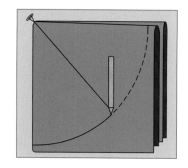

Needle Felting

Visit leisurearts.com to view a short needle felting Webcast.

Apply wool felt appliqués, yarn or roving to background fabric using a needle felting tool and mat (Fig. 1). Lightly punch the needles through the wool fibers and background fabric to interlock the fibers and join the pieces without sewing or gluing (Fig. 2). The brush-like mat allows the needles to easily pierce the fibers. We used the Clover Felting Needle Tool to make our projects—it has a locking plastic shield that provides protection from the sharp needles. Felt, wool and woven cotton fabrics all work well as background fabrics.

Fig. 1

Fig. 2

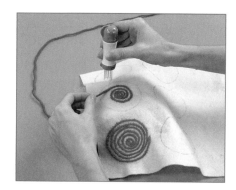

Embroidery Stitches

BLANKET STITCH

Referring to Fig. 1, bring the needle up at 1. Keeping the thread below the point of the needle, go down at 2 and come up at 3. Continue working as shown in Fig. 2.

Fig. 1

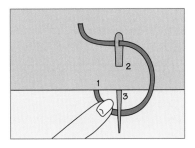

Fig. 2

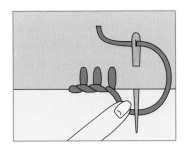

CROSS STITCH

Bring the needle up at 1 and go down at 2. Come up at 3 and go down at 4 (Fig. 3).

Fig. 3

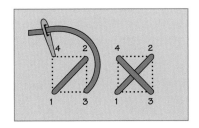

For horizontal rows, work the stitches in 2 journeys (Fig. 4).

Fig. 4

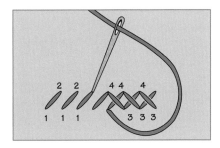

FRENCH KNOT

Referring to Fig. 5, bring the needle up at 1. Wrap the floss once around the needle and insert the needle at 2, holding the floss end with non-stitching fingers. Tighten the knot; then, pull the needle through the fabric, holding the floss until it must be released. For a larger knot, use more strands; wrap only once.

Fig. 5

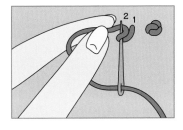

RUNNING STITCH

Referring to Fig. 6, make a series of straight stitches with the stitch length equal to the space between stitches.

Fig. 6

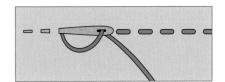

STEM STITCH

Referring to Fig. 7, come up at 1. Keeping the thread below the stitching line, go down at 2 and come up at 3. Go down at 4 and come up at 5.

Fig. 7

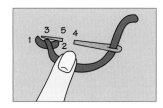

STRAIGHT STITCH

Referring to Fig. 8, come up at 1 and go down at 2.

Fig. 8

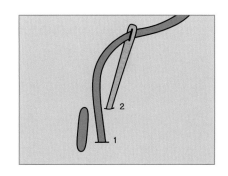

WHIPSTITCH

Bring the needle up at 1; take the thread around the edge of the fabric and bring the needle up at 2. Continue stitching along the edge of the fabric (Fig. 9).

Fig. 9

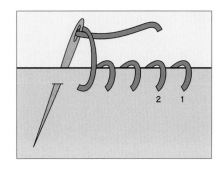

Pom-Poms

For a 2" diameter pom-pom, place an 8" piece of yarn along one long edge of a 1"x3" cardboard strip. For a 1¹⁄₂" diameter pom-pom, use a ³⁄₄"x3" strip. Follow Fig. 1 to wrap yarn around and around the strip and yarn piece (the more you wrap, the fluffier the pom-pom). Tie the wound yarn together tightly with the 8" piece. Leaving the tie ends long to attach the pom-pom, cut the loops opposite the tie; then, fluff and trim the pom-pom into a smooth ball.

Fig. 1

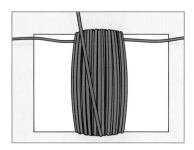

Working with Jump Rings

To open a jump ring without putting too much stress on the ring, use 2 pairs of needle-nose pliers to grasp each side of the ring near the opening. Pull one set of pliers toward you and push the other away to open the ring. Work the pliers in the opposite direction to close the ring.

Knit

ABBREVIATIONS

cm	centimeters
K	knit
mm	millimeters
P	purl
PSSO	pass slipped stitch over
st(s)	stitch(es)

★ — work instructions following ★ as many **more** times as indicated in addition to the first time.
( ) or [ ] — work enclosed instructions **as many** times as specified by the number immediately following **or** contains explanatory remarks.
colon (:) — the number(s) given after a colon at the end of a row or round denote(s) the number of stitches you should have on that row or round.

GAUGE

Exact gauge is **essential** for proper size. Before beginning your project, make the sample swatch given in the individual instructions in the yarn and needle specified. After completing the swatch, measure it, counting your stitches and rows or rounds carefully. If your swatch is larger or smaller than specified, make another, changing needle size to get the correct gauge. Keep trying until you find the size needles that will give you the specified gauge.

CHANGING COLORS

When changing colors, always pick up the new color yarn from **beneath** the dropped yarn and keep the color which has just been worked to the left (Fig. 1). This will prevent holes in the finished piece.

Fig. 1

KNIT 2 TOGETHER
(abbreviated K2 tog)

Insert the right needle into the **front** of the first two stitches on the left needle as if to **knit** (Fig. 2); then, **knit** them together as if they were one stitch.

Fig. 2

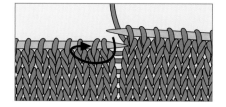

PURL 2 TOGETHER
(abbreviated P2 tog)

Insert the right needle into the **front** of the first two stitches on the left needle as if to **purl** (Fig. 3); then, **purl** them together as if they were one stitch.

Fig. 3

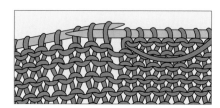

Slip 1, Knit 1, Pass Slipped Stitch Over

(abbreviated slip 1, K1, PSSO)

Slip one stitch as if to **knit**. Knit the next stitch. With the left needle, bring the slipped stitch over the knit stitch (Fig. 4) and off the needle.

Fig. 4

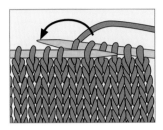

Picking Up Stitches

When instructed to pick up stitches, insert the needle from the **front** to the **back** under two strands at the edge of the worked piece (Fig. 5). Put the yarn around the needle as if to **knit**; then, bring the needle with the yarn back through the stitch to the right side, resulting in a stitch on the needle. Repeat this along the edge, picking up the required number of stitches. A crochet hook may be helpful to pull the yarn through.

Fig. 5

Weaving Seams

With the **right** side of both pieces facing you and edges even, sew through both sides once to secure the seam. Insert the needle under the bar **between** the first and second stitches on the row and pull the yarn through (Fig. 6). Insert the needle under the next bar on the second side. Repeat from side to side, being careful to match rows. If the edges are different lengths, it may be necessary to insert the needle under two bars at one edge.

Fig. 6

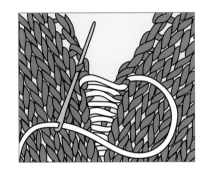

Crochet

Abbreviations

ch(s)	chain(s)
mm	millimeters
Rnd(s)	round(s)
sc	single crochet(s)
st(s)	stitch(es)
YO	yarn over

( ) — work enclosed instructions **as many** times as specified by the number immediately following **or** work all enclosed instructions in the stitch or space indicated **or** contains explanatory remarks.
colon (:) — the number(s) given after a colon at the end of a row or round denote(s) the number of stitches you should have on that row or round.

Markers

Markers are used to help distinguish the beginning of each round being worked. Place a 2" (5cm) scrap piece of yarn before the first stitch of each round, moving marker after each round is complete.

Joining with Sc

When instructed to join with sc, begin with a slip knot on the hook. Insert the hook in the stitch or space indicated, YO and pull up a loop, YO and draw through both loops on the hook.

Reverse Appliqué Table Runner
(page 19)

Bell & Tree Silhouettes
(page 28)

Santa & Sleigh Tray
(page 30)

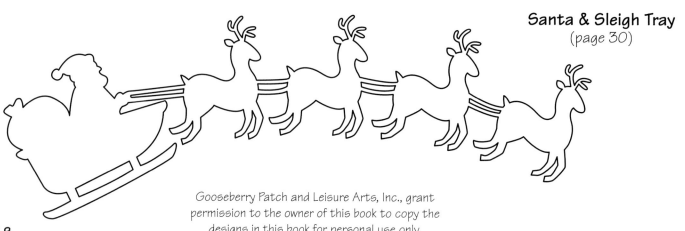

Girl & Tree Silhouette
(page 26)

Santa Silhouette
(page 27)

Santa Globes
(page 28)

Tree Topper Felt Ornament
(page 33)

Pincushions
(page 52)

Felt Ornament
(page 33)

Felt Ornament
(page 33)

Mini Stocking Garland
(page 43)

149

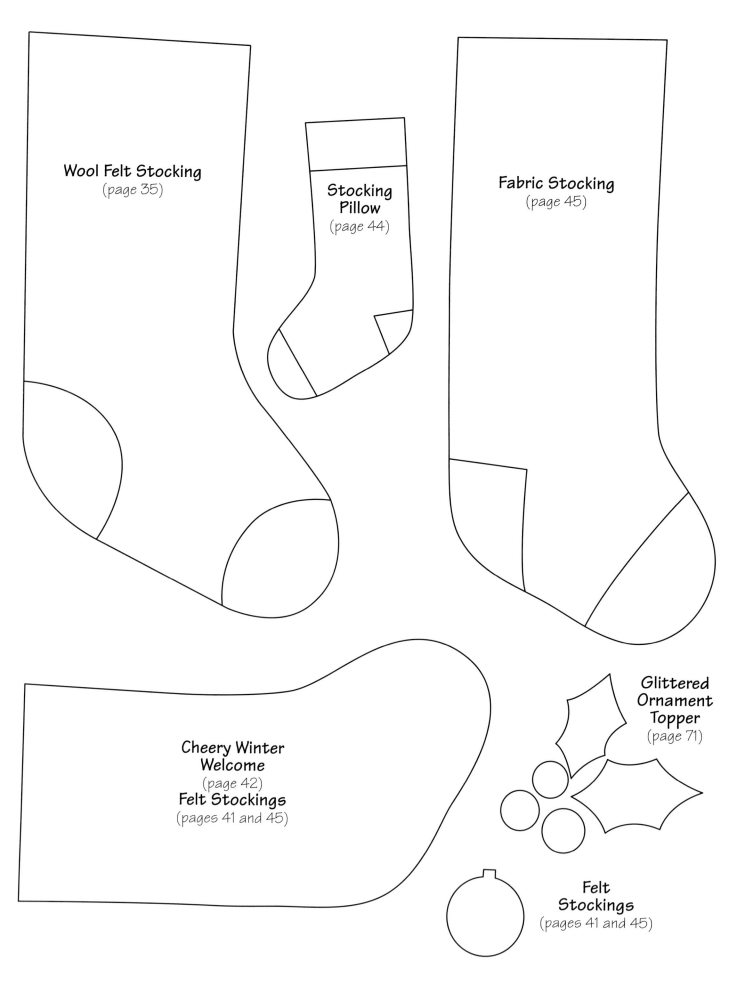

Wool Felt Stocking
(page 35)

Stocking
Pillow
(page 44)

Fabric Stocking
(page 45)

Cheery Winter
Welcome
(page 42)
Felt Stockings
(pages 41 and 45)

Glittered
Ornament
Topper
(page 71)

Felt
Stockings
(pages 41 and 45)

Frosted
Jars
(page 37)

Button & Felt
Flowers
(page 53)

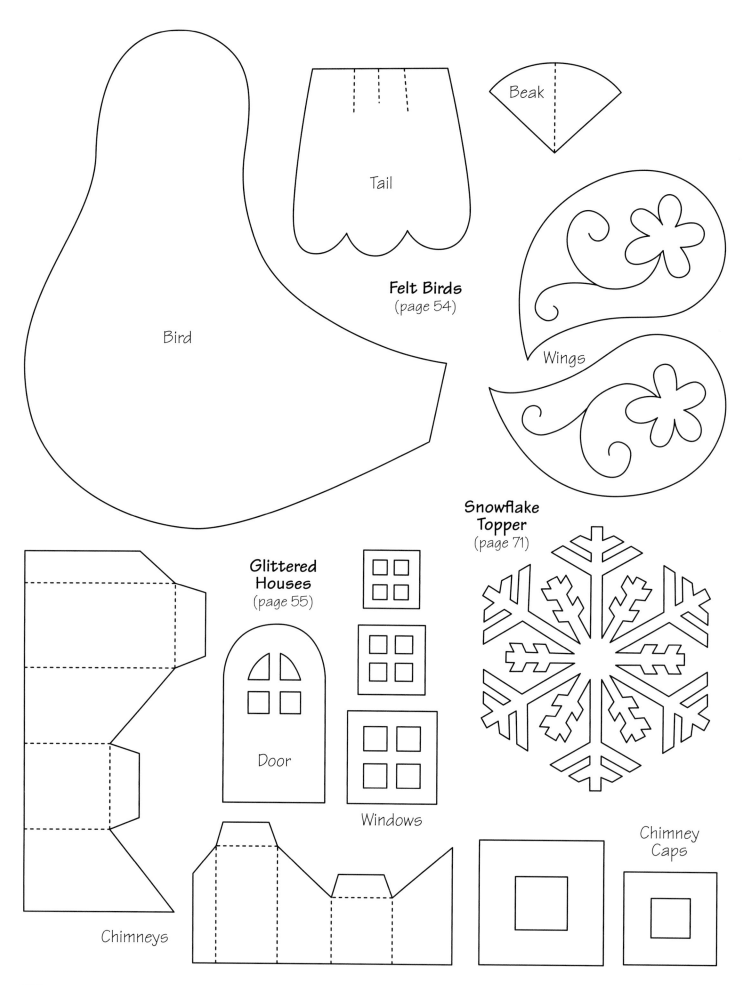

Tail

Felt Birds
(page 54)

Beak

Bird

Wings

Snowflake Topper
(page 71)

Glittered Houses
(page 55)

Door

Windows

Chimney Caps

Chimneys

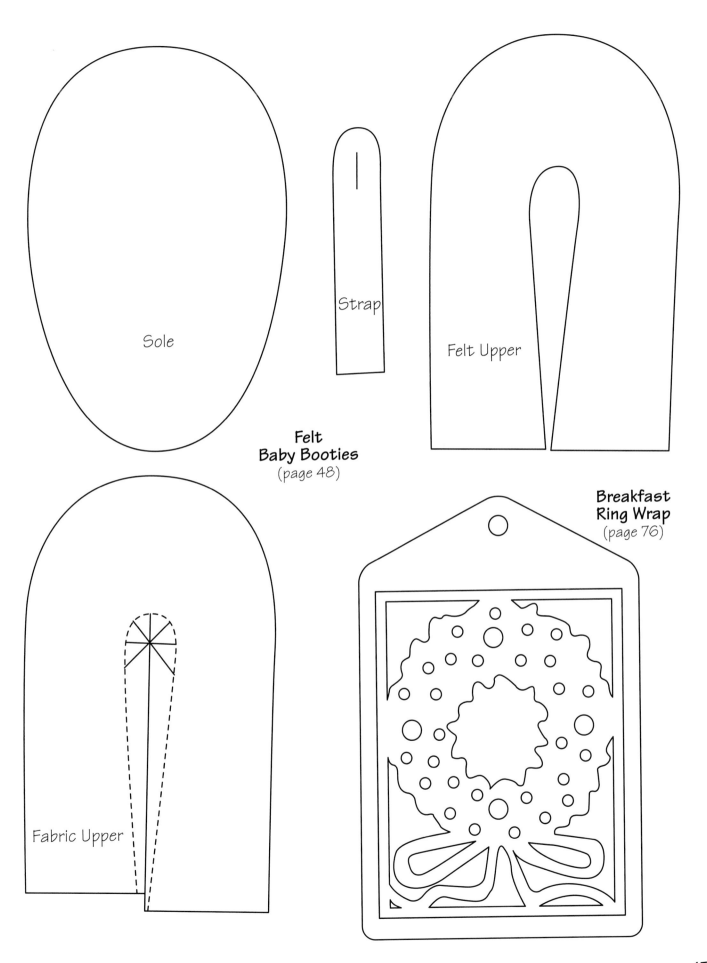

Sole

Strap

Felt Upper

**Felt
Baby Booties**
(page 48)

Fabric Upper

**Breakfast
Ring Wrap**
(page 76)

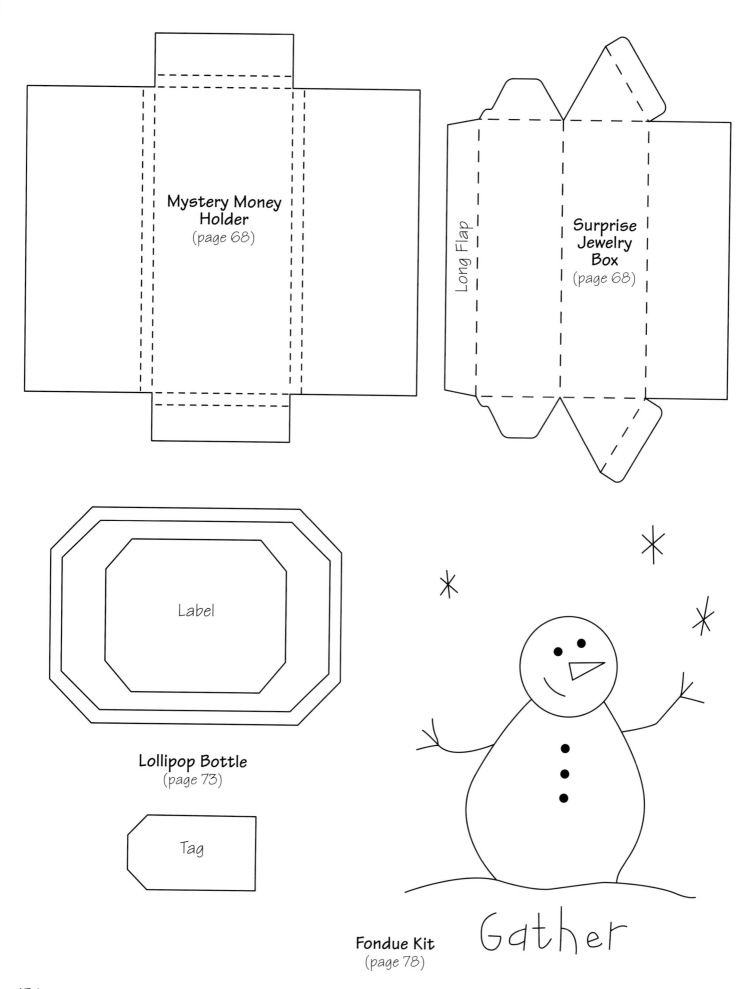

Mystery Money Holder
(page 68)

Surprise Jewelry Box
(page 68)

Long Flap

Label

Lollipop Bottle
(page 73)

Tag

Fondue Kit
(page 78)

Gather

Bottle
Opening

Cookie Holder

Cookie
Window

Flap

**Cookie
Holders**
(page 83)

Valance

Label

Muffin Box
(page 78)

Muffin Box
(page 78)
Cupfuls of Truffles
(page 79)

Pour ⅓ cup
of mix into a mug.
Add ¾ cup boiling water
and stir to dissolve.
Enjoy!

Cocoa Jars
(page 75)

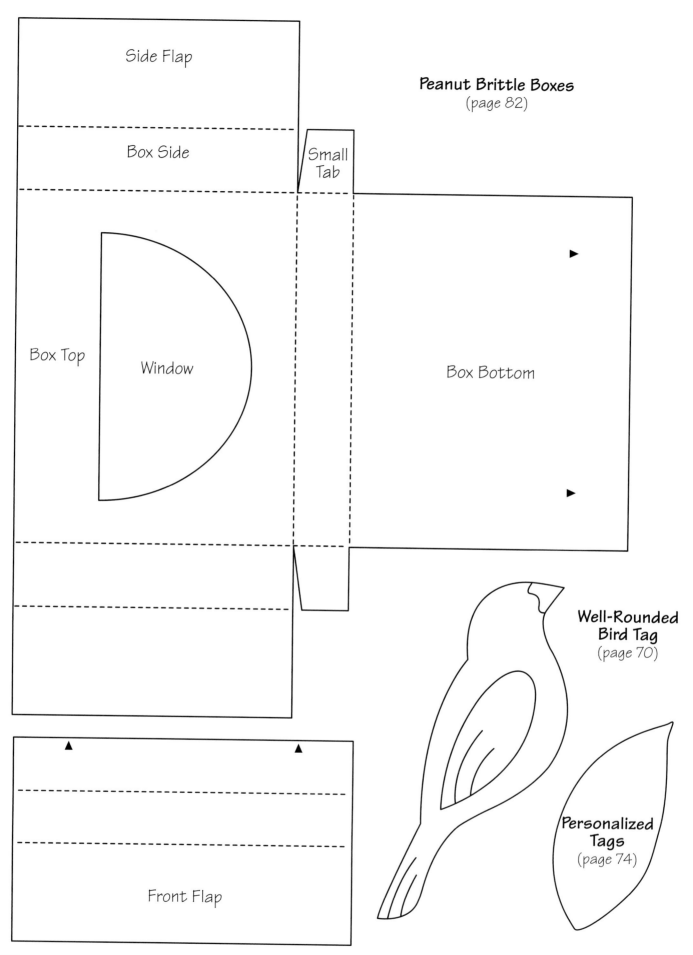

Side Flap

Box Side

Box Top

Window

Small Tab

Peanut Brittle Boxes
(page 82)

Box Bottom

Well-Rounded Bird Tag
(page 70)

Personalized Tags
(page 74)

Front Flap

The family is one of nature's masterpieces.

Santayana

Project Index

Recipe Index

Credits

We want to extend a warm "Thank you!" to the people who allowed us to photograph some of our projects at their homes: Nancy Nolan, Nancy Porter, Jacob Rice, Angela Simon and Emily Thom.

We want to especially thank Mark Mathews of Mark Mathews Photography for his excellent work.

We would like to recognize the following companies for providing some of the materials and tools we used to make our projects: Lion Brand® Yarn Company and Caron® International for yarn, Saral® Paper Corporation for transfer paper, The DMC Corporation for embroidery floss, Raggedy Junction for Meltie Felties marbleized wool felt and Clover Needlecraft, Inc. for the felting needle tool, mat and mesh transfer canvas.

For the use of the live tree on page 33, we are grateful to Arkansas Plant Brokers of Little Rock, Arkansas. The sweet kitten on page 58 visited us from the Humane Society of Pulaski County in Little Rock, Arkansas.

Special thanks go to Raymelle Greening and Margaret Taverner for knitting the Knit Pillow and Knit Stockings. We also thank Paula Vaughan for the use of her photo technique in the Portrait Silhouettes.

If these cozy Christmas ideas have inspired you to look for more Gooseberry Patch® publications, treat yourself to a Gooseberry Patch product catalog, which is filled with cookbooks, candles, enamelware, bowls, gourmet goodies and hundreds of other country collectibles. For a subscription to "A Country Store in Your Mailbox©," visit www.gooseberrypatch.com.